Reflections

Reflections

STAATSBURG: "NOT JUST A PLACE TO LIVE"

A Collection of Interviews with Community Members

Conducted, Transcribed, and Edited by
Judith Linville

Epigraph Books
Rhinebeck, New York

Reflections: Staatsburg: "Not Just a Place to Live": A Collection of Interviews with Community Members © 1986, 2019 by Judith Linville

All rights reserved. No part of this book may be used or reproduced in any manner without written permission except in critical articles or reviews. Contact the publisher for information.

ISBN 978-1-948796-70-5

Book design by Colin Rolfe

Epigraph Books
22 East Market Street, Suite 304
Rhinebeck, New York 12572
(845) 876-4861
epigraphps.com

Table of Contents

List of Photographs VII
Preface to the New Edition IX
Preface XI
Acknowledgments XII
Introduction XIII
Charles Kendall 1
Lucile Hayes 15
George Forman 27
John Van Dyke 45
Naomi Craft 59
Edith Kidder 66
Kenneth Stewart 73
Birgit Crusius 89
Leonard Peluso 94
Marion Asher 102
Oliver Goring 110

List of Photographs

Fourth of July Parade passing the intersection of Old Post Road and Mulford Avenue in Staatsburg, New York X

Diving at "Little Norrie Park" on the Hudson River, Staatsburg, NY 5

The beach at "Little Norrie Park" on the Hudson River, Staatsburg, NY 8

Charles Kendall 11

"The Locusts" estate of William Dinsmore 14

Class picture from the Staatsburg School 16

"The Locusts" estate of William Dinsmore in Staatsburg, NY 19

A Hudson River Dayliner passing the Little Norrie Park 34

Two Staatsburg residents 44

Farm workers from Enderkill Farm at the Ogden Mills Estate 46

Harvesting ice from the Hudson River in Staatsburg, New York 54

"Staatsburgh" the home of Ogden Mills 57

Gardens at the Dinsmore Estate 60

Greenhouses at the Ogden Mills Estate 65
Family in a car in Staatsburg, New York 68
"The Point" estate of Lydig Hoyt in Staatsburg, New
    York 71
Basketball game at Staatsburg School 75
Wooden schoolhouse next to a new Staatsburg
    School 87
Dr. Herridon on Old Post Road in Staatsburg,
    New York 90
Intersection of Mulford Avenue and Old Post Road in
    Staatsburg, New York 93
Fundraiser billboard for ambulance in Staatsburg,
    New York 100
Staatsburg Train Station (smaller of two
    stations) 106
Schouten's Meat Market on Market Street,
    Staatsburg, NY 108
Norrie Point Restaurant on the Hudson River,
    Staatsburg, NY 117
Sign for the Civilian Conservation Corps Camp at
    the south entrance of the village of Staatsburg,
    New York 118

VIII   Reflections

Preface
to the New Edition

After many years, *Reflections* has been re-published and is now available on-line, in a paperback format. It is my hope that this will allow more readers to learn about the bygone days of Staatsburg , a small village located on the Hudson River between Rhinebeck and Hyde Park, New York and it will cause readers to reflect on what home means to them.

Well researched historical data can provide factual information about a community's past. But, if the right questions are asked and one listens quietly, the true heart of any place will be revealed through the recollections of those who live there. Such is the case with this book.

All of the people originally interviewed on these pages have since passed away, so their stories have become more poignant and more invaluable as they tell about living and working in Staatsburg in the early and mid-1900s. Although historical accuracy may be sometimes lacking, the rich memories and perceptions captured here are irreplaceable.

Each narrative helps to define "community" in its most universal sense. Combined, the stories remind us of what we hold dear no matter where we live.

It was my privilege and a true honor to know these delightful people and to see my hamlet, Staatsburg, through their insightful eyes.

Judith A. Linville
May 2019

Preface

The following manuscript is a collection of edited narratives based on tape-recorded interviews about the people and area of Staatsburg, New York. It focuses on the period of 1910 to the 1960s. This hamlet in the Hudson River Valley had experienced economic prosperity from approximately the early 1800s up through the 1930s, due in large part to the influence of seven major, contiguous estates along the river. As employers and benefactors, or merely by their physical presence, wealthy landowners affected many of the people whose memories are recorded here.

The residents of Staatsburg experienced sociological as well as economic upheaval due to a series of complex, but inter-related factors. The Depression, two world wars, the decline of Albany Post Road as a major highway through the hamlet, a reduction of public transportation, and an end to the era of the great estates all contributed to a profound change of lifestyle for the people of the village.

The oral histories in this collection tend to be biographical in nature because the emphasis is meant to be on the relationship between "people and place." Just as the school, parks, estates, river, and national events influenced the children and adults living in Staatsburg, so in turn did the people, because of who they are and where they came from, create a community.

    Judith A. Linville
    Staatsburg Oral History Project

Acknowledgments

Thanks are extended to all the individuals and organizations who contributed moral or financial support to this project.

Special thanks go to: Spackenkill School District for a half-year sabbatical leave from my teaching position; the Staatsburg Library Society for their sponsorship; Dutchess Community College for use of the Norrie Point facility; Pamela Wolven for her excellent advice and typing skills; Frederick A. Nero, Sr. for his guidance with the printing process; Ned Leadbitter for graciously sharing his slide collection; and Bob, Benjamin, and Cortney for their love.

Of course, my deepest appreciation goes to the narrators who took the time and interest to give me their personal reflections.

Introduction

Staatsburg, like many other areas in the Hudson River Valley, was once the home of wealthy, aristocratic families who came here to spend their leisure time. Langdon, Thompson, Dinsmore, Mills, Hoyt, Livingston, and Norrie are some of the gentlemen farmers, industrialists, and politicians who chose this part of Dutchess County to maintain either a year-round or a part-time residence.

Between 1715 and 1720, the first prominent citizen of Staatsburg bought property from the Pawling Patent and settled on the land that would bear his name. Dr. Samuel Staats was a respected physician with six beautiful daughters who became the belles of society in Dutchess County and married well-to-do men.

However, this is not a story about money or prominence or the landed gentry. It is, instead, reflections of ordinary, hard-working people who came to Staatsburg for reasons that are as varied as the people themselves. Most of all, it is a story of individuals and families who shaped a way of life in a small hamlet.

During their lifetime, they saw great changes in the nation as well as in the village. But they adapted to change with humor and resilience. Here they tell of childhood, family life, and building a community that is more than just a place to live.

Although this is not a story about the people who lived on the estates, it is about individuals who are wealthy, indeed. For in these memories which they have shared, we see the special pride, loyalty, and love of people who took just a place to live, and made it a place that we call home.

XIV   Reflections

March 1987

Charles Kendall

I met with Charlie over the course of several evenings to conduct this interview, but it should be noted that his interest and efforts in the preservation of Staatsburg's history have extended over many years. He and his wife Audrey raised five children in their home on Baker Street and contribute a great deal of time to community service.

Charlie Kendall appears to be a quiet and reserved man, but he is characterized by a wide grin, a sharp wit, and most of all a fierce loyalty to the village where he has lived all his life.

"The days that make us happy make us wise."
–JOHN MASEFIELD

DURING MY CHILDHOOD, I lived in eight different houses all over Staatsburg. I was born in 1922 in the house just this side of the Hyde Park Nursing Home on Route 9. When I was about five we moved from Staatsburg to Florida where my father was hoping to find work. But he was killed in a car accident shortly after we got there. That left my mother with me and my sister, Alyda, who was six at the time. That was 1927 or 28 and my mother came back to what she knew. She had a sister in Staatsburg.

Those were tough times. It was the Depression, and we were basically poor. My mother worked many jobs and many hours. I can remember her working six or seven days a week just trying to make ends meet. It was "stay ahead of the landlord." I think part of the reason we moved so much was the landlord wanted the house for someone else or for various reasons.

We were aware of the Depression as kids. You knew you were poor and there were some better off than you. And you certainly knew there was money and you didn't have it. We qualified for welfare and one of the things I remember as a welfare recipient is that they would give you clothes, but they gave the same type of clothes to everyone. One thing they gave you was corduroy knickers—all the same color—your basic gray. When you had those gray corduroy knickers on, they all knew you were poor and on welfare. They called them "whistle britches." You always got that little jab from someone at school because as you were walking down the hall, the corduroy would rub together and make a whistling noise.

I was not the only poor kid in school during that time; there were lots of us. There were certainly more poor than wealthy. There were probably just a few wealthy people in town and rest of us were average or below.

I started kindergarten in the old wooden school on Old Post Road. I remember outdoor johns and I remember more than one class in a room with a divider between. Once, my sister's class was on the other side of the divider and I heard her teacher telling them all about the trips they were going to take to France and England on their imaginary geography trips. Well, I took that all to heart and really and truly believed that my sister was going to leave. I remember going to my mother very upset that Alyda was going to leave!

In the brick school, all the elementary classes were on the first floor, and the second floor was grades seven through twelve. One of the great experiences in that school was when you went from grade six to seven, you climbed those stairs. That was the "forbidden territory." The only thing up there was the nurse's office, the principal's office, and the seventh graders and up. So once you went up those stairs, you were one of the big kids. That was one of the things you always remembered about school.

Eva Kuhn and Mrs. Hayes were two of my teachers. There were only two principals while I was there—Irwin Baker and Gaylord Hakes. Ken Stewart came as a coach and then later became principal. If you had a sport, he coached it.

I left school just before the war broke out and went into the service when World War II started. After the war, I went back to Poughkeepsie High School and got my diploma in 1946. Quite a few of us in town went back to high school after the war. You went to school in Poughkeepsie, but you got your degree from Staatsburg School.

We heard about Pearl Harbor at Mass in St. Paul's. It was sort of the talk of the town that Sunday morning. The next day two of us went down together to the Poughkeepsie Post Office to enlist. Pearl Harbor was close to home, and most fellas didn't need flags to be waved.

Jimmy Schulhoff and I went to join the Navy. His father was a retired Navy man, and we knew we were going into the Navy. Well, when we got there the Post Office was packed with fellas.

The line to the Navy recruiting office was a mile long so we decided to walk around for awhile and maybe come back tomorrow. As we walked by one doorway, we looked in and saw this huge man sitting behind a desk. He looked up and saw these two young faces.

"Can I help you?"

"No, we're just waiting for that line to join the Navy to get a little smaller."

This giant stood up in a beautiful blue Marine uniform and said, "YOU'RE GOING WHERE?? Step inside and let me tell you a little story."

If you don't think Jimmy Schulhoff had some job telling his father that we signed up to go into the Marines and that he wasn't going to be a Navy man!!

After getting my high school diploma, I went to Farmingdale on the GI Bill. Jack Dugliss and I went down together. We lived in dorms the first year, but after that we had the first house trailer on campus. I met Audrey by then. In fact, Tom Steenson's girlfriend from Rhinebeck had introduced us the night I graduated from Staatsburg School. That was in 1946 when we started going together.

I came back to Staatsburg after college because my family was here, Audrey was in Rhinebeck, and because Staatsburg was home. I probably could not have thought of a better place to live. And I'll tell you some reasons why.

The most interesting part of growing up in Staatsburg was certainly Norrie Playground down on the river. There were two sections at Norrie—the beach part where the younger kids were, and the dock section where the older kids were. The beach was south of the parking lot. It was about 40 yards down the path where there's a steep embankment. There were steps that took you down to the beach area, and there was a float out in the water for the bigger kids to swim out to, dive off, hang around, show off, I suppose. As a kid you stayed in this beach section until you were able to swim, and you had to prove to Bart Hinds that you were able to swim good enough to "graduate" from the beach to the dock section. 'Course that was a big point in your life when you went to the dock. You were one of the big kids. You were one of the River Rats.

Mr. Hinds was the supervisor at the park. He was a tyrant, but it was for our own good, although it was hard for us to realize it at the time. There was the usual horsing around, but not too much because he'd stop it.

The dock was at the foot of the hill as you came down the road into Norrie Playground, on the right-hand side. It had a sliding board, a diving board, and a lower and higher diving tower. After you got to the dock, you went through various steps of accomplishment. First it was going off the diving board, then the lower tower, and the ultimate of course was going to the high tower. It was quite a thrill—it was high and you were swimming in water with tides and currents, so you could have a six-foot tide. The current wasn't too bad and you could use it to your advantage. If you wanted to go from the dock to the beach section, it was a lot easier if there was a down tide.

The real crowning point of your childhood was when you were sixteen or seventeen and tried to swim across the river. It was one mile across with tides and currents, so when you did it, you picked the right time to swim. You swam as close to ebb tide as possible so that the water was pretty much at a standstill. Very few people attempted to swim across without a boat nearby. Bart Hinds would never have allowed it. That, without a doubt, was probably the greatest day of your life—when you swam the river.

There was a man, Jimmy Ellsworth, a steelworker who was probably the strongest man that lived in Staatsburg. He would come down to that dock after working all day, stand and loosen himself up a little, and then dive in and swim by himself to a dock across from Norrie. When he got over there, he'd wave his arms to us and then stay and rest for a little while. Then he'd dive in and swim back across the river! I was able to swim across, but I never would have attempted to go over and back. That's exhausting.

One area I've spoken about before is the city people who came up to stay at the boarding houses and thought that everyone up here was a country bumpkin. Well, we probably were but we certainly weren't as dumb or naive as they thought we were.

My favorite story was about going to the ball games in Staatsburg where the town teams played each other. It was good baseball and every Sunday the boarders from Stone's Farm and Whitewall Manor would come to the ballpark for something to do and to watch the "farmers" play ball. Some fellas from the village would sit in the stands and look at the railroad signals up on the tracks. When the signal arm would go up, they'd look at their watch, and if it was 2:14, Joker Rowe would call up to Harry Stickle, "The 2:17 should be here pretty soon." Sure enough, within a few minutes you'd hear a whistle and the 2:17 would be coming through town. Perhaps a half-hour later, the signal arm would go up again from the other side, and Harry Stickle would yell down to Joker Rowe, "Gee, the 2:45 should be coming." Sure enough at 2:45 a train went by. That seemed to amaze the city people to think that with all the trains that go by here these people knew every train and every time that it should be going by.

I remember the trains stopping in the village. That was probably a big part of your growing up—getting down close to those monsters and seeing them. 'Course, then they were steam locomotives with all the cinders and the noise, and the grinding of the wheels and the steam. Certainly as a child that was a great experience to stand by those monsters.

There was a man at the crossing all the time in those days who put the gate up and down. In fact, he worked the gates manually. There was a tower and he would watch for the signals. That would tell him to put the gate down. We always crossed there back and forth on our way to the river.

There were some things you did, when you look back at it now, that were dumb. And I'll tell you the dumbest thing that the kids used to do down at Norrie. Again, this was for the pleasure of the city people. The Dugliss fellas were great for doing this; they were super swimmers.

You'd line up a couple of guys on the dock who would start talking for the benefit of the city people.

"How long do you think you can hold your breath underwater today?"

"Well, I think probably about three minutes."

"C'mon, you can't do that. You've come close, but you've never actually made three minutes."

"Yeah, but I think I can do it today. I think I can hold my breath for three minutes underwater."

Now, the city people knew no one could hold his breath that long, but little did they know that some of the timbers under the dock had eroded away, and so had some of the earth under the dock. So, the kid whose turn it was to "hold his breath for three minutes" would dive in and then go under the dock and put his head up into this little space which formed an air pocket. "Then he could hear the kids up on the dock go through the whole thing. "He's down there for a minute...a minute and a half...My God, he's going to make three minutes!" 'Course the city people would think he was drowning. Then the dummy under the dock would come out and put on an Emmy award exhibition of how you should look if you've been under water for three minutes. Actually, he could have stayed down there long enough to write a novel.

There were a lot of barges filled with bricks that went up and down the river. One of the fun pastimes was to row a boat out to a barge, pull up behind it, and go up on the barge. They were going slow, anyway, being pulled by tugboats. You'd take some bricks (borrow some bricks); they had a barge full of them, they weren't going to miss a few. You'd bring them back to the dock and distribute them to the River Rats. Then you'd take something sharp and somehow chisel your initials in the brick. You would hide your brick anywhere in the dock area—bury it in the mud, or stick it up under the

timbers in the dock—anyplace that you thought nobody would find your brick. You sort of became, well, the longer your brick remained hidden, the better you were. Sometimes you'd go down very early in the morning before anyone else was there and pick out the spot to hide the brick. There were boathouses down there and a cement ramp to launch boats, and that whole area was where you hid bricks. They were simple games, but important to kids.

I can remember the Mills Mansion in the wintertime. You could go sleigh riding on their hill even when the family was there. What they would do was put lanterns out at night on the riverside of the mansion so you could sleigh ride at night. Then you could go down those steps to the basement area and the cook or butler, or whatever he was, would give you hot chocolate and cookies. We were always skating on Mills Cove. That was probably the greatest place for people to skate because the ice was smooth and it was easy for people to get to. Iceboats were quite common, too. Well, the rich people had iceboats, and some people in town had iceboats. The Gilberts from Hyde Park were great iceboat people.

It's strange how you remember things like this. Of course, a great hill to sleigh ride down was Mulford Avenue from Route 9. If the conditions were right you could really fly, and the kids used to invite the teachers out to sleigh ride at night. You had an opportunity to see them in an entirely different context. In school it was strict, but Weltha Robinson—give her a sleigh, a gang of kids, and a lot of laughter, and you saw an entirely different person.

Something that was just fading out when I was very young was bobsledding. The Kidders and Chuck Burke tell stories about riding a bobsled down Mulford Avenue, but they would start across Route 9 all the way at the top of Prospect Street by the huge oak tree. This would have been in the late 1920s so there weren't many cars on

Route 9 at night. They said they would come down Prospect, across Route 9, and they would still be going at the four corners in the village where they would take a left and go past the firehouse!

There were always fights in those days. Every day there was a fight in the village. Kids would fight, but it was nothing for grown-ups to be fighting—go into a bar, get into an argument, go outside and pound each other. Physical fights. I think it had to do with the competitive situations people were caught up in. If there was a job opening, there were probably ten people trying to get that job, so it was all tied in to that desire to get something; and if someone got in your way, you just pushed them aside. I doubt very much if boys today have had that much physical contact. With us it was literally an everyday affair, and there was always an area in town where you fought—behind the firehouse, on the fifth tee on the golf course, or behind the school. I don't know if it was a way to relieve yourself or express yourself, but everybody fought. And you know, you could fight Bill Smith today and tomorrow go swimming with him. It didn't seem people carried a grudge—it was just to get those anxieties out of your system.

Everybody had a bike of some kind, but I never had a new bike. You either got one that had been someone else's, or you got one that you could fix, but a bike was a big part of your childhood. It was probably more important to a kid in those days than a car is to kids today. There were only two wheels and you had to pump them, but it sure saved you from walking to the river!

The golf course was a source of income for us because you could caddy for the millionaires. The entrance and first tee in those days was across from where the Hayes house is now. It was strictly a private golf course owned by the Dinsmore family. A good many people thought that Ogden Mills owned it. Probably because his estate was closest to it and because the Mills mansion was more of a partying mansion than the Dinsmore mansion. You'd go to caddy early on Saturday, and there was a man, Alvia Horan, in charge of the course, who would keep a tight rein on the kids who'd showed up to caddy. When the entourage would come out of the Mills Estate—now this could be eight or nine or even ten big touring cars—you'd head for a car to get their bags for them  so you could caddy. You sort of fought for the bag, but if you made too much of a fuss, Mr. Horan wouldn't let you stay. He wouldn't let you caddy for a week or two. Now there were certain fellas in town who were permanent caddies. Some people had had these kids for years as their own personal caddies, but then there were all the Mills's guests who needed caddies. Of course, all the wealthy people used that course—the Astors, the Vanderbilts, the Dinsmores.

If you were picked, they would pay 50 cents a round for a single bag and you could also carry doubles. You got 75 cents for doubles, and in those days it was only a nine-hole course. It was more fun on Sunday morning because they usually came out after a party the night before and they were still feeling pretty good. They would maybe get half-way around the course and decide they were not going to play anymore, so they'd head back to the car, but you got full pay and an extra tip if they were still tipsy themselves.

'Course there was always the golf ball that would go into the rough. It was your job, as caddy, to go and find the ball. It depended on who you were caddying for and how smart you thought they were. You'd go over and think, "Gee, that's a brand new ball he's got there, and if I find that ball, the ground is nice and soft and I could step on the ball and push it down into the ground, and I'll remember where it is, and I'm gonna come back here tonight and dig that golf ball out of there." That's how you got a golf ball on the millionaires. They wouldn't have any patience. You'd look around in the rough a little while and say, "Sir (or ma'am) sorry, I couldn't find it." They'd tell you to just take another ball out of the bag so they could continue to play.

It was wrong. You were stealing. But you didn't think of them as missing anything like that. They were rich and you were struggling, so a golf ball was worth another—I forget, maybe a quarter—to you. You'd take them home, clean them up, and take them back to the golf course to sell.

The course was private and the local people couldn't use it on weekends or when the wealthy people were here, but William Dinsmore saw to it that the local people could use the course through the week. I don't remember if they even had to pay, but as long as the millionaires weren't using it, Staatsburg residents were allowed to use that course. The Dinsmore people were marvelous people, to my recollection. They were more out of the partying limelight. Mills has the name, but Dinsmore was the one who did the most for the community.

It seemed to me that when William Dinsmore wanted to get rid of the golf course—they all wanted to get rid of their mansions and estates when they started to have to pay taxes on them—that he turned that golf course over to the village of Staatsburg. I say this and other people tell me I'm crazy, but it seems before the Taconic State Park

Commission got a-hold of it, William Dinsmore had actually deeded the course over to the village of Staatsburg.

The Dinsmores lived at "The Locusts." In those days it was the big old wooden house. The Dugliss's father apparently had something to do with the Dinsmore Estate. Three or four of us would go over to the Dugliss house in the evening and we would walk with lanterns to the Dinsmore house. Sometimes there would be ten or twelve of us, and I don't know how we got there because that would mean we walked through the Mills property and the Hoyt property. God, we didn't walk the railroad tracks; there must have been a path through the woods. But we'd get to the Dinsmore House and Mrs. Dinsmore would have a movie screen up in the trees on the south side of the mansion. She would sit in the window and all of us—Mr. Dugliss and all the kids—would sit against the foundation of the house. They would project a movie up on the screen, and she had a little speaker that came outside so we could hear. There was a time, between movies or at intermission, when the butler would come out and serve milk and cookies to us.

I remember Mrs. Dinsmore more than anyone because she always came to the window to welcome us when we got there. And when the movie was over, she'd come to the window again and we'd step back from the house a little and look up and say, "Thank you very much, Mrs. Dinsmore."

"You're welcome, children." And off we'd go. Not many people remember that.

William Dinsmore was probably the most important part of this whole community. Hyde Park had basically three wealthy families—the Vanderbilts, the Rogers and the Roosevelts. But I think the wealthy in Staatsburg gave more to Staatsburg. For example, for the size of this town, they never would have had that firehouse if it wasn't for the Dinsmore money. Dinsmore gave them the land and financed the biggest part of the building of the firehouse. And it was one of the only ones in New York State to have a bowling alley, when bowling alleys were something only wealthy people had. When the firehouse was built, it was built with good money. I mean it didn't go out to low bid!

It was the same thing with the school. I truly believe that Staatsburg, for its size, had no right to have a beautiful school like that. It was a poor community coming out of the Depression. It was built primarily with Dinsmore money. He gave the land for the school to the people of Staatsburg. I think there was a certain amount of jealousy on the part of Hyde Park many, many years ago because of what Staatsburg had.

Dinsmore had that ball field built. It was regarded as one of the finest ball fields between New York and Albany. He brought the man who designed the Polo Grounds in New York up here to look at that field. There's actually a complete drainage system under that ball field. Mr. Dinsmore gave to the community.

July 1986

Lucile Hayes

Mrs. Hayes is a spirited eighty-three-year-old woman who has an excellent memory for details, and a warm, sincere personality. We met for the interview in her house on Route 9G, where she proudly showed me pictures of her children, ten grandchildren and eleven great-grandchildren.

Although not a native of Staatsburg, Mrs. Hayes agreed to talk about some memories of the village from her perspective as a schoolteacher and the wife of a life-long resident.

Like all good storytellers, Lucile Hayes possesses both the ability to laugh at herself and a decided twinkle in her eye.

"How vast a memory has Love..."
—ALEXANDER POPE

I CAME FROM GROTON, CONNECTICUT, to Staatsburg in 1927 to teach in the wooden school across from the brick school that now stands. Let's see, the first year I got out of college, I taught in Hurleyville, New York, and one year was plenty long enough there! Then I stayed home one year and worked in the school office in Groton. My friend, Frances York, who taught second grade, got a job in Staatsburg through an agency. She worked for four years and then wrote and told me about a teacher leaving to get married. There would be a vacancy in third and fourth grade—why didn't I apply? So, I applied to the Staatsburg School.

I came for an interview in February and it was cold with lots of snow on the ground. There was lots of snow in those days. Mr. Baker had started that year as principal, and he took me up to see Harry Barker who was in charge of hiring teachers. Couldn't hire a teacher unless Harry Barker said it was the right one. Harry Barker did not like short hair on women. In those days, you wore hats summer and winter. I had on a big, black velvet hat with embroidery on the brim. Mr. Barker walked across the room and took that hat right off my head to see if my hair was short or long. I was so mad at him! It didn't make me very happy, but he did it, and then he hired me and I came to work in the fall of 1927.

When you came into Staatsburg, you came on the train, and the first thing you saw when you got off was Bodenstein's Tool Factory and Kidder Coal. There was Hughs's Store—the big brick building by the tracks. When I first came, it was the only store, and what a good

GRADE 3 and 4   MISS DAVIS (Teacher)

16   Reflections

business he did, too. They sold everything in there. They had a good meat department and food downstairs. Upstairs he had cooking utensils. And he delivered, too, you see. I brought my kids in there to buy them arctics. In those days they didn't have boots—they had galoshes or arctics. Next to Hughs's was the post office and next to that was Millard's Confectionery Store. He sold good candy—not penny candy, good candy. He made wonderful ice cream sundaes and sodas. He was a little man who was all bent over—he couldn't straighten up. When you walked a little further, you saw White's Plumbing and the old Route 9.

I lived in Markle's house on Mulford Avenue—second house up from the brick house on the corner. The present Harry Markle's father and his wife took teachers in. Boarding was common; there was no place else to live. Well, you know that hotel on the corner was a nice place in those days. Some of the teachers lived there. In fact, Margaret Quinn, who married my husband's brother Ed, was a schoolteacher from upstate and she lived in that hotel. In Markle's house I roomed with my friend, Frances York, but she was not a well person and she had to leave Staatsburg. Then I went to people by the name of Pavitts. That was the last house on the left going up Hughes Avenue. For our meals we went to Mrs. White's which was the house kitty-corner across the street. In the springtime I was sick and my parents came here and took me home. While I was home, Mrs. Pavitt wrote to tell me they were moving to Poughkeepsie, so I went to live with Mrs. Briggs up the hill on Elm Avenue when I came back. It was a nice place to live. Boarding was nice—you had home atmosphere.

The children were very good. They weren't rowdy like they are today. That's not a very nice word to use, but I don't know how else to express it. They behaved themselves, and too it makes a big difference what kind of teacher you are. I discovered very early in teaching that if you scream and yell at them they're not going to behave. You know how I used to calm them down? I'd stand in front of them with my hands behind my back and I'd just about whisper to them. They'd look at each other, and then they'd look at me and quiet down because they didn't want to miss anything, you see.

I had thirty-five students in third and fourth grade. That wasn't too bad. I taught one year in Clinton Hollow—six grades in one room—a wooden, one-room schoolhouse. It was up a road that was on the left just before you came to the store in Clinton Hollow. I had one student in sixth, no one in fifth, and grades one and two and three and four were combined. The girl in sixth grade was so smart I hardly had to tell her what lessons to do; she just did them and got them right. I really felt sorry for the girl because I couldn't spread myself between the other four grades without her doing that. They closed that school. The children didn't have anything to work with and it was on a side road away from everything. The kids had to walk in all kinds of weather. It was time that school was closed.

In the Staatsburg school I had one student I remember very well. She didn't do her work. She did not pass third grade, and I would not pass her on to the fourth grade. They told me I had to. I said I won't pass her; I just won't do it. That didn't set right. Harry Barker said she had to go into the fourth grade, and when I came back in the fall, she was sitting in the fourth grade. I said, "O.K., if you're going to be in this grade, you're going to do all of the third grade work, too." And I told her mother that. Every night she went home with all that third grade work, and she had some fourth grade homework—she wasn't as quick as the others. That did her the world of good. It worked beautifully. And she told someone—it pleased me greatly—that that was the best thing that ever happened to her, that I wouldn't let her go into the fourth grade without doing the third grade work. That's the only time I had a pupil compliment me.

I was teaching in Staatsburg when I met my husband. I'll tell you how I met him. I knew who he was and he knew who I was. The big deal in the evenings was to go to the post office. It didn't close until 7:30 p.m., and when the last mail came in it was sorted and you went to see if you had any mail. So one night I went to the post office and Marty was standing outside. When I went by, he said, "Good evening, Miss Davis." I stopped and talked to him and that was the beginning. No formal introduction—everybody knew everybody in the village. I lived at Markle's and he lived in the Hayes's house. My husband's name was Martin William Hayes and he was named after his second cousin, Martin William Hayes.

The Hayeses worked on the Dinsmore Estate. Grandfather Hayes was a shepherd. They had a lot of sheep at one time. Across the street from the Hayes's on Old Post Road, at the exit to the Mills Estate, there was a great big sheep barn and an enclosure for the sheep. They

would let them out in the spring, summer and fall when the grazing was good. Sometimes they even let them on the golf course if no one was playing golf. And that's how Grandfather Hayes came to be here. Grandmother Hayes was a cook. Could she make good biscuits! I tried my best to make biscuits like she did, but I couldn't.

When I was going out with Marty, he had no car. His brother did, but his brother was courting someone at the same time so the car was always being used. We'd go down to Poughkeepsie on the train. It was a lovely train station we had here. It's a crime they tore that down. There was an underground tunnel, you know. It went from the east side to the west side so you wouldn't have to walk across those tracks if you didn't want to. It's a shame. That was a nice building that could have been made into something.

In the 1930s there were a lot of trains. Why, you could go to Poughkeepsie four times a day. Marty and I would go to a movie, go out and have a treat, and come back on the train at 10 o'clock at night. There was the Bardavon Theatre, and a nice little theatre on Liberty Street. There was another small theatre up Main Street. Sometimes we'd go down in the afternoon, go around the stores, and then we'd go to dinner. There was a restaurant—oh, you'd know it if I could tell you. I had it in my mind a minute ago and it just popped out. Isn't that funny? Smith Brother's Restaurant! Also, there was a hotel on the corner that had a nice little restaurant. There were buses to Poughkeepsie, too. They ran every day of the week but Sunday.

There's no trains and no buses now. I drive very little any more. I go from here to the Episcopal Church in Hyde Park where the senior citizens are. Occasionally, I sneak down to the Grand Union, much to my daughter's distress.

I think Marty and I went together a year and a half before we got married. My parents weren't too happy. I was brought up in the

Congregational Church and I was marrying a Catholic. They thought Catholics weren't any good for some unknown reason. Marrying a Catholic was the most awful thing in the world to do. I was in trouble before I even got started. The night before I was going to get married, I called my parents up and my father wanted Marty and I to come to New York City because he wanted to meet Marty. Well, after he met Marty he felt very much better because Marty was a very pleasant person; a very nice person if I do say so.

So, a brother of Marty's came over from Waterbury with his girlfriend and we went down to the rectory of Regina Coeli Church in Hyde Park. I could not be married in St. Paul's in Staatsburg because I wasn't Catholic. We were at the old Regina Coeli and the old rectory that faced Harvey Street. They should never have torn that little brick church down. It was a very pretty place. I can't remember the priest's name. He was a little bit of a man. He was full of pep, and he was a nervous wreck. He ran upstairs and downstairs in the rectory, "I can't find my book! I can't find my book!" I wasn't nervous a bit, but he was a nervous wreck. That was 1930. I was married on the 14th of June. I had been boarding with Mrs. Briggs. After we were married, I went back to Mrs. Briggs's and stayed, and Marty stayed at home. And then as soon as school was over, I moved in bag and baggage with the Hayes's.

I lived in the brick house next to the Catholic Church in Staatsburg for seven years after we were married. We moved in on August 1. It belonged to my father-in-law. He owned half of Staatsburg at one time. He owned the house on the west side of Dr. Herridon's house, and all that corner lot, and he owned a lot of land. You know they wanted to put Grove Street all the way through from Elm to Mulford, but my father-in-law owned all that yard, and he put that brick house up way back there so they couldn't put the road through. I liked that house. It had a beautiful porch that came from the back door all the way across the front and up the west side of the house to where that window is bowed out. It was wonderful when my kids were little. I'd put gates up. We had a gate by the backdoor and one on the east side so in the wintertime I could put the kids out in the sun in the morning. It was a beautiful house inside, too.

When I moved to Staatsburg in 1927, there were the Hoyts, the Dinsmores, and the Mills. The Hoyts was in full swing; The Dinsmores was kind of half-and-half, and the Mills, well for a little while someone lived in the Mills Mansion, but then they turned it over as a museum. It's not a home. Like Vanderbilts down there—it's beautiful but it's not a home. They had big greenhouses at Dinsmore's. They had a big one at Hoyt's, too. Ray Baright worked there. And they had a big one at Mills's. Naturally, Marty went to work at the Dinsmores because Dinsmores liked the Hayeses and they said if he wanted a job, he could have one there at the greenhouse. Marty loved flowers! He graduated from Eastman College, but he didn't pursue his profession. He liked the flowers.

The Dinsmores used the flowers in the greenhouses just for themselves. They had big parties on the estate. They were very kind to their help. I'll never forget it as long as I live! Every Thanksgiving and every Christmas they'd give their employees a turkey. Well, the first time I got a turkey, Grandma Hayes said to give the turkey to her, she'd fix it for me. She had no confidence in my ability to clean a turkey. Well, I don't know as I could have! I didn't even know how to start a turkey, so she showed me how to clean it and I did my own after that.

I remember I was married and lived in the brick house, when Martin Jr. was five and Laura was a tiny baby, Marty came home one day and said, "Well, Ma, I'm gonna have no job soon."

I said, "How come?"

"Dinsmores is closing up!"

That was, oh dear...well, 1936. He didn't know what he was going to do. He went all over and he couldn't find a job. Cousin Mart had a friend in Rhinebeck—that lawyer, Frost—the old man, the original Frost—and he wrote a letter to the state hospital recommending Marty to work there. In those days he had to work nights for six months as a watchman. He had to go from one building to another and punch a clock. When the six months were over with, he got into the greenhouse and he was there almost thirty years. In the summertime in those days they had beautiful flower gardens all over the hospital grounds, too.

It was terrible the way they carried on in Staatsburg at Halloween. They did all kinds of things! There were no inside bathrooms in that old wooden school; it was outdoor johns. One for the boys and one for the girls. Every Halloween those johns were tipped over. Also, when poor old Mr. Millard got so he couldn't take care of the candy store anymore, somebody else took over. The kids evidently didn't like this man who took it over. Came Halloween time—I'll never forget it as long as I live—I stood next to my daughter Laura, believe it or not, and she was throwing rotten apples at him. I near died!

Next to the post office on Old Post Road is a big house. It was in beautiful condition at one time. An old lady by the name of Washington lived there. Lord, she died years and years ago. My son doesn't even remember her and he's fifty-five years old. I remember going there to see her when I was pregnant for Laura. Marty was only four years old. And of all things she insisted on giving me a glass of wine. I almost died before I got home. I can't drink wine; it makes me so sick. I was being polite, but it doesn't always pay. She took charge of a lot of things to do with St. Paul's Church. I think she saw to it that it was cleaned.

Then there was a pair of old ladies—what the dickens was their name? They lived across the tracks down the River Road. They were old maids, and I mean the old-fashioned, old-maidy old maids! One of them played the organ and the other one sang in the choir at St. Paul's. The poor thing—the one that played the organ wasn't too bad—but the one that sang was supposed to be leading the choir and she couldn't carry a tune in a bushel basket. Creeley was their name. There was some very nice homes down where they lived. The road isn't even there anymore.

I remember Dr. Herridon's house on Mulford Avenue. It was so pretty inside. I had their daughter, Mildred, in third grade, and she had an older sister in third year of college. Anyway, the house had this great big foyer, a big living room, and a very big dining room. The doctor's office was down a small hall on the west side of the house Upstairs the master bedroom was right across the front part of the house. I used to go upstairs there because Mildred was in one of our class plays. Every year, each grade had to give a play in the firehouse. Mildred was a pretty girl. And I forget what the name of the play was, but Mildred was a fairy and she was just the right type for a fairy. Her mother was clever making clothes. She made the prettiest fairy outfit—with wings and everything, and I had to go upstairs in their house to approve of the costume and see if it was right and what not. As if I knew how to sew. My mother was a seamstress, but she forgot to give me the knack.

Across from Dr. Herridon's there was some violet houses behind all those houses on Mulford. They were there when I first came to Staatsburg; there were just a few of them and then they disappeared one at a time. They were out in the field. They had to be out in the open so they could get some sun.

The town hall on Mulford was still there when I lived in the brick house, but it was not used anymore. It was kitty-corner across from St. Paul's.

When my girls were little—Laura and Ann—Ruth Baright and I had a 4H in a little room over the barber shop. And I used to take the kids' shoes to the shoemaker's in Staatsburg to have new soles put on. I had his daughter in school. She married Len Peluso.

Oh, and that empty lot on the corner across from the post office—when I first came here, there was a lot of stone piled up there. That lot was filled high. I'm not very tall and I could just about see over the stone, and my husband was almost six feet two and he said he could just about see over it. Somebody was going to build a big hotel and use the stone; that's what was told to me. But then it kept settling and settling. So that's all solid stone underneath that lot where there's grass now.

We had been in the brick house for seven years when Cousin Mart came to Marty one day and said, "I think you ought to have the little house on the corner of Reservoir Road and North Cross Road." It was beautiful up there when we moved in. Uncle Charlie lived just up the hill a ways on Reservoir Road and he had a big farm. He farmed both sides of the road and he owned all the land over there, including the land our house was on. Just like Cousin Mart owned all this land over by 9G, he owned all that over there near North Cross Road.

But the riff-raff, as Uncle Mart called them, moved in. One day he told us he would give us a piece of land here on 9G, but to make it legal we'd have to pay a dollar. So we got 100 feet wide and 100 feet deep all for one dollar because it belonged to Cousin Mart. He owned over by that gravel bank all the way to the "mountain" as we called it—those hills in the back. When I first moved here, I'd go out the back door and walk to the top of those hills; it was all open then. I could look all around. It was beautiful. This house is twenty-seven years old. I have a grandson who was born the very same year. Michael Doyle was born the same year we built this house.

Lucile Hayes   **25**

I know very well I would've never been married if I'd stayed in Groton. I'll never forget when I was about twenty-two years old, a young man I was brought up with—he used to come over when I was about "that high" and take me to school by the hand. His name was Richard Allen and he was one year ahead of me in school. Richard and I were great pals all of our lives. But, when I was twenty-two he called me up one night and wanted me to go out. I was delighted! Dick was the nicest person in the world, you know. Well, Auntie says, "You be home by 10 o'clock." So Dick looked at me and said o.k. We took a ride and he stopped the car. He said he was going to take me to a dance in Wesley, Rhode Island, which wasn't that far from Groton.

I said, "Well, go ahead."

He said, "Oh, no! Mrs. Davis said to have you back by 10 o'clock, you'll be back by 10 o'clock."

Naturally to say, he didn't ask me out again. And that's the way it was with any boy who wanted to take me out at night. When I graduated from the two-year teachers' college in Massachusetts, I ran into a snag. I could teach almost anywhere but Connecticut. My folks were madder than hops. I couldn't teach in Connecticut where we lived. Well, it worked out better for me because I know very well I would've never been married if I'd stayed there.

Marty worked at the greenhouse at Hudson River State for almost thirty years, but then he got sick. He got hardening of the arteries of the brain and became very ill. I couldn't care for him anymore so we put him in Hudson River State as a patient. He was there five years before he died, but he didn't realize where he was. Funny part of it was—he'd go up to the greenhouse and he'd pick up the hose and water the flowers just like he always had when he was working there. They let him do that.

February 1987

George Forman

George Forman is a tall, friendly man who has lived in Staatsburg for fifty-five years. He is a quiet and introspective person, and like many of the long-time residents I spoke with, he has very strong feelings about the village.

As evidenced by his narrative, George and his family had a difficult time during the Depression. But the sense of community and the silent support they received from neighbors, teachers, and friends may help to explain the deep loyalty and fond memories George holds today for Staatsburg.

Stories of childhood mischief and good times on the river are important to George, but he by no means lives in the past. Although he saw Staatsburg during its more prosperous days, George Forman feels optimistic about, and works for, the improvement of the village where he still lives.

"The history of every country begins in the heart of a man or woman."
—WILLA CATHER

THE THING IS, from hearing people talk and looking at all those slides, they showed you a part of Staatsburg with the yachts and everything. Well, there was another part of Staatsburg, too. That's where I came from—the other side. We had four children in our family and my father lost his job during the Depression, so it was pretty rough through the 1930s.

We moved here in 1932 when I was seven years old. My parents were from Staatsburg, but they had moved to Mechanicsville when my father had gotten work on the railroad. When he lost that job, we came to the village and lived with my grandfather in the fourth house down from the corner on Old Post Road. My father found a job here but it wasn't too great a job. He worked at the farm down at the Anderson School. He made $25 every two weeks and we had six people in the family. That was for about four years and then things started picking up a little bit, and he got a better job. My father was a carpenter by trade.

It was tough. I know lots of times we went hungry. The worst part I remember—well, when you're a kid, you know, kids adapt to things, but I remember a lot of times my mother crying trying to figure out what we were going to eat from one meal to the next. To tell you the truth, I really don't know how she did it. She used to make all homemade bread. It wasn't easy, that's for sure, but that's my worst memory from the Depression.

Along the same lines, there were people like Jackie Dugliss's mother and Mrs. Kidder, Mrs. Radcliffe and different people in the village who, whenever we went out to play, always made sure they had something to eat for us. So, people made sure they looked out for you. I don't know, I think it carries over today. You don't forget that—people like that. There was a closeness. People didn't look down on you. It was just a closeness there. And we all got along well together no matter what we had. I don't think it hurt us any. I think probably we were better off—I don't know.

We liked school when we were kids, the Staatsburg School was good. In fact it was brand new when we came in 1932. You went in one side and came out the other side twelve years later. The teachers were all pretty good to us. The teachers knew we were one of the poorest families in the village and they kind of took care of us; made it a little easier on us. Some of them were pretty good, too. Each fall the teachers would come back and stay with a different family. Some would stay on Old Post Road with Mrs. Kidder, or with Mrs. Radcillfe, who had the fifth house up from the corner, or with Mrs. Morris who lives where Bob Gaudier lives now. Most of them were single women and several of them married local guys. Like Mrs. Kuhn married Walt Kuhn and Bud Hess's wife was a teacher—her name was Evelyn Day. Freddie Kidder's wife taught down there, too.

One thing I remember about going to school in Staatsburg is I have an older brother—well, I had, he's dead, now—but he was about four years ahead of me and all we ever heard from the teachers was, "Why can't you be like your brother?" He was a real good student.

I was a good student until I got into high school and then I slacked off quite a bit. I was trying to be an athlete! There were so few kids when I got to high school that we all had to play on the basketball, baseball, and football teams. We didn't have much choice; we had to play otherwise there wouldn't have been a team. Mr. Stewart used to call us in and say, "You guys have gotta play." He didn't give us much choice.

Mr. Stewart was tough but he was good. I don't think there's a kid who went to school down there who doesn't like him a lot. He was fair. I know when my father took us down to register for school, he told the teachers, "You're in charge when they're here—whatever you have to do." And if they did have to do anything we knew we were going to get it again at home, so I think that made the point a little better. I think most people had respect for education.

I remember when we had an assembly the principal would read out of the New Testament or Old Testament. I was thinking about that—they would never do that today.

We used to have to go out and cut wood every day in the winter to keep the fire going at home. We would take the cross-cut saw and the axe and cut down trees. When I was about ten or eleven years old, we were cutting a tree down and my grandfather's dog was with us. The tree fell on the dog and killed him. We were afraid to go home. My grandfather wasn't too happy.

When we were in high school, we worked on a chicken farm in Rhinebeck during the summer. That was around the early 1940s and we worked for a man named Rupert Shook. He was the nephew of Jake Rupert, the beer man. They had about 35,000 chickens and the first year I worked in the chicken houses. We had to clean out the cages—it was not a nice job. I didn't eat chicken for quite a few years after that. Then we worked out in the fields. We took in the hay and stuff like that. When we brought in a load of hay up there he always had beer for us. Plenty of Rupert beer!

Around Christmas time the Methodist Church in Staatsburg always had a party. Even though we didn't go to that church, Mrs. Dugliss used to take us over there for candy and an orange. She always took care of us real well, and you never forget a thing like that. I know we would walk up to midnight Mass with my mother every year. Up at St. Paul's. It would be real cold. Then when we got older, like in high school, we always went over to Sinibaldis after midnight Mass. To the house on Mulford Avenue where Tony lives now. Their family always had a big party after Mass—spaghetti, cookies, and all kinds of good things. They always had a full house.

We palled around with Tony Sinibaldi. He was a few years younger, but he was a big kid and he always hung around with us. There was Anna, and Josie, and Angie. And there was myself and my twin brother and Bobby Simmons—he died. Billy White was killed in the Battle of the Bulge when he was 18 and a half years old. We all hung around together. We had gone to school together from first grade right on through high school. In the summer we'd play softball and stuff, go swimming. We were always pretty close.

Another thing I was thinking about was the state road—Route 9—used to be like a boundary up there between the village and out there. There used to be a fellow named Bill Mahar who lived over on 9G. On Saturday he would come in to the village to go to the store and we'd chase him all over the village. Poor guy. Just because he didn't live in the village, we'd chase him all over the place.

The Episcopal Church would have a Strawberry Festival on Flag Day, June the 14th. We used to help them set up the chairs on the lawn and they'd give us a piece of strawberry shortcake. Some of the women would have a special topping they'd pour over it—that was delicious.

We used to go up to the estates. I remember when Mrs. Dinsmore lived up where Bob Guccione lives now. She lived in the old house, the great big one. She used to have two huge trees on the south side of the house. They would put a big sheet up between the trees and show movies. And whenever Mrs. Dinsmore would show movies, they would send word down to the village—to the kids. We would take blankets (it was usually in the fall), sit out on the lawn, and watch the movies. I saw "Treasure Island" for the first time up there. The first time I saw that movie. She would sit out on the porch and we would sit on the lawn. She would have quite a crowd up there.

I remember Mills's. In the summer, on a hot day, we'd go down there and hang around their icehouse; chop some ice off and eat it. My grandmother worked in Mills's kitchen. I don't remember her because she died when I was quite young. But my mother told me that Mrs. Mills always left orders—if anybody came to the door, they were never to turn them away. There were a lot of hobos in those days walking up and down the railroad tracks. So the Mills were pretty generous people. I also remember my mother telling me that a couple of times Mrs. Mills would be down at Hughes's store and she would take the kids inside and buy them rubbers if they didn't have any for the winter.

In the fall, the Mills family would come up to play golf, and when they came to play golf, they wouldn't come alone—there would be about 15 or 20 people with them. We used to watch for the cars. They had the big Rolls Royces and we could see them leave the big house to go to the golf course. Then a gang of us would try to caddy for them. Usually the bigger kids got the jobs first, but if they had a lot of people with them, we'd get a job, too.

The thing I'll never forget is some of the language on the women! They'd hit a bad shot and they had pretty good language on them, I'll tell you. This one guy, John Kuhn, whenever Mrs. Mills wanted him to caddy for her, she'd get him right out of school. She would request him and they'd let him out of school. Very few people around here played golf. They couldn't afford to. Just the rich people played.

We used to go up to fish off the Huntington's dock and we'd swim down at Hoyt's dock. Nobody ever minded. We could usually walk all over the estates.

There were Brothers from Mt. Saint Alphonsus, across the river. They had oceanliner lifeboats and it would take about six guys to row them. They'd row all around the river on those boats and sometimes during the summer they'd come over and spend the day on this side of the river—swim and play ball with us. We would just happen to come by at lunchtime and they'd feed us. We usually always knew when it was lunchtime! They were good guys.

That park down at the river was our lifesaver. We used to spend all summer down there. We'd go down in the morning, take a lunch, go home for supper, and go back down and stay 'til dark. We had a lot of fun down there. A lot of good times.

I remember the tides would change every six hours. Sometimes if you were out in the river swimming against the tide, you'd go no place. We used to swim across the river with a guy in a rowboat next to us. If you started at the dock at Norrie Park, you could wind up about two miles down the river if the tide was going in a certain direction. You had to e a good swimmer and swimming across the river was part of "belonging." If you couldn't do that, well....

We had this thing we used to do, especially on the weekends when we had a big crowd. We used to dive off the dock and there was an opening underneath the dock where you could breathe. So we'd dive off and then go up under the dock. A couple of kids would say, "What happened to him? What happened to him?" People would get really worried about what happened to us. That was one of our favorite tricks.

We used to go out to the barges that would go up and down the river with bricks. We'd take some bricks and each kid would carve his initial in one. Then we'd throw them in the river and try to find our own bricks. That was kind of hard sometimes—at high tide it was dark down there! Usually we liked to swim when the tide was up because it was a lot cleaner. At low tide there was seaweed and stuff in there. Mr. Hinds was the supervisor down at Norrie, and he was tough. I know he yelled at me more than once. I remember one time—we used to have knotholes in the girls' bathhouse—and I was looking in when I heard, "REDHEAD!!" I looked around and I knew who it was. It was Bart and boy did he let me have it!!

It was usually a tight ship down there. We could never go swimming alone or anything. You never went swimming alone. Bart was the lifeguard, and if you couldn't swim, he wouldn't let you go off the dock. He would send you down below to where they had the beach and the float. You had to prove to him that you could swim well enough for him to let you go to the dock.

At the dock there was a sliding board and two diving towers—a lower one and a higher one. The higher one was probably fifteen feet or so. As a kid, it was a big thing, you didn't really belong until you could dive off that high tower. We would go up there and stand maybe a half an hour trying to work up the nerve to go off. But if we did that, my older brother and a couple of the other bigger guys would come up the ladder, and they wouldn't let us down, so we had to go off.

We had a lot of traffic on the river, too. The big dayliners would go by—the Robert Fulton, Henrik Hudson, and the Peter Styvuesant. Two of them would go up and back down every day. That used to be one of our big things. We had to get down to the river by one o'clock because that's when the first dayliner went up. They made big swells and we wanted to be swimming when they went by. That was one of our timetables. We had to be there then.

During the summer we'd go down to the park on our own, but there were a lot of organized activities at Norrie, too. The churches would have their days down there—swimming races and picnics and things like that. Anyone outside the village who wanted to use the park had to get a special permit because the village people had first preference. Outside people were invited to use the park, but they had to make arrangements ahead of time.

Every weekend it was crowded with families. They used to have a guy who came down with an old truck with canvas sides on it. He would sell candy, ice cream, and soda. Frozen Milky Ways were the big thing. If we got one of them, it was great—made our day.

The river is still there now, and the park is such a beautiful spot. It's just too bad it couldn't be back the way it was. I think it's cleaner now than it was when we swam in it.

During the Depression there weren't too many good moments, but down by the river we had fun—all kinds of good times.

I really couldn't tell you for sure, but I think the heyday of Staatsburg was probably before the 1930s, maybe the 20s and before. And I think after Route 9 stopped going right through the middle of the village, the heyday started going down. At least from what I heard from my mother and father and grandfather. Route 9 was being built around the village when we came here in 1932.

On Market Street I remember Hughes's store. It was a general store. He sold refrigerators and stoves and things like that in there. There was Johnny Millard's ice cream store and another grocery store near Millard's. Sam Schouten's Meat Market was on the corner of Market Street and Railroad Avenue. When we were kids we used to go up to the golf course and hunt for golf balls. We'd take them down and sell them to Sam Schouten. Next to the meat market was the rectory for the Methodist Church, and then came the church.

Across from the present Post Office is an empty lot and it has always been empty since we moved here. Across from the library on Old Post Road was a restaurant, but I forget the name of it.

We had a corner tavern on the corner of River Road and Railroad Avenue. We used to hang out there after high school. We used to have a lot of fun. It was a busy spot. The railroad station was still open then and people would get off the train and stop in the tavern. First it was called the Corner Tavern and was owned by a family from Poughkeepsie named DiGilio. Then Eddie Green ran it and Steve Talebar ran it after that. I think he was the last one.

Then we had the Cardinal Inn on Old Post Road, which was run by Paddy Hart before it was the Cardinal Inn. That was a busy, busy place. Then Herman Boucher ran it and they had a very good family place in there. Up on Route 9 where Paula's restaurant is now, there was another tavern. We would go up there after a basketball game or something when we were in high school. They had a jukebox and we'd dance and have a couple of drinks. We didn't have to have a card to get a drink the way the kids do today. At least they never asked us for any—as long as you behaved yourself. They knew who you were.

We also went down to the Cozy Inn where the bait and tackle shop is now on Route 9. Down below that was the Staatsburg Tavern. That was run by Bud Hess and it was a busy place. But they were all pretty busy. The Green Bullfrog was just south of the Staatsburg Tavern. Both those buildings are gone now. You know, most of these places lost a lot of traffic and business when the Taconic Parkway went through. Before that, Route 9 was the main road from New York to Albany.

We never went to Stone's Farm very much, but we did go to Whitewall Manor in the summertime. They were boarding houses across form each other on Route 9. A lot of people from New York City would come up for the summer, and Whitewall Manor would hold dances in their big barn. It was a recreation hall. We had a lot of fun in there. A lot of boarders were cops from New York City who would come up for the summer.

The ice tool factory was a big thing going in Staatsburg in those days. Sometimes we'd go in and sit down in the summer and talk to the guys who were working. That was an awful hot place to work. They'd have these furnaces next to the machines and they would be stoked with coal and they would be hotter than heck. They had to take the ice tools and put them into the fire to get them real hot so they could bend and shape them the way they wanted them.

The amazing thing about this factory was everything was run by pulleys. There were big leather pulleys going all over the machines. They had what were called trip hammers to pound things into shape. It would be quite a racket. When the doors were open in the summertime, you could hear it from quite a distance.

My grandfather worked down there for a few years. He was a tool and dye maker. They shipped all over the world, I guess. They made marlin spikes and those ice carriers that looked like great big scissors. And one guy down there, John Ostrander, invented creepers that strap on to your shoes or rubbers. They had real sharp points on them for walking on ice. Those were sold to the general public. When we used to have snowstorms in the village, they would plow the snow into great big piles, especially over in the area by the stores and the post office. They didn't have any backhoe or anything to pick the snow up, so if you were over sixteen years old, they'd hire you to shovel the snow onto the trucks—one shovelful at a time. We'd load those trucks by hand and that's how we'd get the snow out of town. But we didn't mind. It was something to do.

The estates, as far as the people in the village were concerned, were like an industry because half the people in the village worked on the estates at one time. I remember when Mills gave his property over to the state. It didn't have much effect on me. Lydig Hoyt closed later on. He gave his property over to the state, too. I remember when Mrs. Dinsmore sold. She was a nice woman. As a matter of fact, all of them were nice—fairly good to the people in the village. Morgan Hall, over on River Road, burned right down to the ground. It had been bought by Anderson School and was being used as a girls' dorm at that time. That was a beautiful building. It sat back in the woods and had all the English ivy all over it. My uncle used to drive for Morgan as a chauffeur for a few years. This had been more or less their spring and fall house.

Doc Herridon was a real nice guy—a tall thin gentleman with rimless glasses. I remember one time I had a blister that got an infection and I went to his house on Mulford Avenue where the office was. He started right in on the blister—no anesthesia or anything. I can still feel it. It healed it, though!

We were playing football down alongside the firehouse. This was before we were in high school so we didn't have any equipment or anything. My brother threw a flying block at me and I came down and landed right on my mouth. Three teeth went right through my lip, and they had to bring me over to Doc Herridon's. He took a few stitches in it. He was the emergency room in those days.

Another story I remember about Doc Heridon, which I probably shouldn't tell. We used to hang around the firehouse a lot. This is after we were all out of high school. The tavern closed at two o'clock and we used to get a few quarts of beer and go over by the firehouse to finish off the night. Well, this one night there were quite a few of us. Some of them usually didn't hang out with us and it would end up with a little bit of a fight. Well, this one guy fell down on the floor on a broken beer bottle and he was knocked out. Now this was three or four o'clock in the morning. We had to go over and wake up Doc Herridon. Boy, we were afraid to go over and do that. But he came. By the time he got there, the guy had come to. The doctor didn't appreciate that!

Even though Franklin Roosevelt lived in Hyde Park, it's only four miles away and he had an impact on Staatsburg. He used to come up there and ride around in his old Ford touring car. That car is in the garage at the Roosevelt Library now. It had special equipment for him because he didn't have use of his legs. The Ford agency down in Poughkeepsie and a mechanic down there designed the levers on the steering wheel so he could drive it himself. He'd ride around with the top down. He seemed like a pleasant man. He had a big, hearty laugh. When I was a kid I had bright red hair the color of a carrot, you know—a real, red brick top, and my face was full of freckles. I remember when I'd go by Roosevelt's car, he'd rub the top of my head. You remember stuff like that.

When we moved down here it was in the summer of '32 and he was elected in '32. We lived very near the firehouse where you voted, and I remember all the excitement when he got elected. They had the torchlight parade that went from the Town Hall in Hyde Park to the Roosevelt Estate. Once it was evident that he was elected, he would come out on the porch and the whole family would be with him. I think it was 1940 or 1944 that the Vassar Glee Club was down there to serenade him on Election Day.

And I remember Eleanor Roosevelt did her own shopping down at Lasher's Meat Market in Hyde Park. She was very pleasant, also. She used to write a column for the newspapers called "My Day" and a lot of times she'd write about people in Hyde Park. Each time there was a re-election, the Poughkeepsie paper would write about the local people who would be attending the Inaugural Ball. 'Course there were people around here who hated the Roosevelts—you either hated them or you loved them.

That was one nice thing. In all my twelve years of school, he was the only President we had so I didn't have to remember too much about Presidents. I think I liked him for that. But I know my grandfather and I used to get into some arguments. He couldn't stand Roosevelt because he knew him personally and he always thought Roosevelt was a snob. Well, he was from a wealthy family and we used to argue over that.

During the war they had an MP unit stationed at the Rogers' Estate in Hyde Park. They used to have these little guard shacks along Route 9 with MPs posted in them so nobody could get onto his estate. That was during the war.

I remember when Mrs. Roosevelt died, they had five President here on the day of her funeral. Just seeing the power and the important people who came down here was something. I was always greatly impressed, and I still am today. I think it's great to live in the same town a President lived in.

I got out of high school in 1944. Right out of high school I went to work at Western Printing and I was there for 39 years. All the guys I palled around with went into the service. Like my brother was in the Marine Corps, and Skip Horan was in the Air Corps. He was shot down over Germany and was a prisoner of war for two years. That's Dick Horan's brother.

I couldn't go in because I have a bad eye. I can't see out of my left eye. That was a tough time in my life—seeing all the guys go off and I couldn't go. I took a lot of abuse from different people around here. The funny thing was, when the guys came back, it was just like nothing had happened. There was no resentment from them that I didn't go. We just took up right where we left off before they went away. It was a tough two years, I'll tell you that.

In Staatsburg we had the airplane watch up on the hill on Mountain View Avenue. During the war they used to man that for 24 hours a day to watch for airplanes going over. If you saw one, you called it in. I think everybody was involved in that.

And they had the scrap drives—iron and whatever. They used to take the metal down on the empty lot across from the post office and then when we got enough they'd send a tractor trailer truck up to take it away. Used to get quite a pile, too. They had paper drives and a Victory Garden. The people used to plant their gardens over by the Scout House on Old Post Road. It was more or less a community garden, and each person had his spot. I don't know why they called it a Victory Garden, really.

A lot of changes came after the war. Several of the fellows who went to the war came home for a month or two and then went off to different parts of the country because they had a whole new outlook on life after the war. The skills they had developed during the war—there was more opportunity for them outside of Staatsburg than in the village. My brother went away to college on the GI Bill of Rights. I think quite a few of the guys did that. Some of the kids who wouldn't have otherwise been able to go to college—this was a good opportunity for them.

I think the town declined gradually. I guess the taxes were so overwhelming for the estates that they decided they just couldn't keep them for the part-time, limited use they used them for. So they turned them over to the state.

Then the railroad stopped stopping in Staatsburg. We used to be able to take a bus to Poughkeepsie, and the bus came right through the middle of the village. But they stopped that.

When Johnny Millard died, somebody took over the ice cream store, but it was never the same and it closed.

For awhile in the 40s, right after the war, they used to have dances at the firehouse. The fire company would put on dances a couple of times a month—square dances. They used to get a pretty good crowd. In fact, that's how I met my wife. She used to come up from Poughkeepsie to visit her brother and his wife. They brought her to a dance at the firehouse, where I met her.

When I was first married we lived in Hyde Park for five years. Then we moved back to Staatsburg. I don't know why we moved back—it was like home, I guess. It was like home, and my family was still here and my wife's brother was living up here at the time. I never got too far away from Staatsburg.

I think my best memories—like when we first moved down here from Troy, which was a city, we lived right across from the ball lot. I was so impressed with all the wide-open spaces and the greenery. It was a beautiful ball lot. For years they used to say it was the best ball field between New York and Albany, and it really was. When we were in high school, we'd take care of it ourselves. In the spring we'd get rid of the weeds and the stones and put the roller on it. I thought that was the greatest place in the world when we first moved down here, and it really was.

That park had bleachers and a score board near the ball field. When we were little kids, it was our job to hang up the numbers on the scoreboard. They would get a good crowd at the games. That was the big thing then. Staatsburg had a pretty good team that played teams all over the county. And there was not T.V., of course, so Sunday afternoon was baseball. Everybody went.

I have a photograph of an old Sucony station that was where the monument is on Old Post Road in the village. I think it was up during the 1920s and the early 30s. I think it closed during the Depression. Then the Staatsburg Athletic Club, that was the ball club, used to keep their equipment in the little building that had been the gas station.

The tennis courts were over in the corner of the park that's near the monument. And in the wintertime they would freeze over with ice and we used to ice skate and play hockey. I remember they had the nets with the big poles, and I ran into one of them and opened up my eye—back up to Doc Herridon!

Andy Kiernan, Walt Cronk, and Frank Stoneman used to sit out in front of the garage that was on the corner of Old Post Road and River Road, next to the firehouse. Any Kiernan knew every license plate of everybody in the village, and they used to kid him about it and try to trip him up. One time they asked him what the license plate number on the fire truck was. He was wracking his mind, but there were no license plates on the fire trucks. They had him going for about a half-hour and finally they told him.

There was a feeling when we were all kids—I didn't realize it then, but I realize it now. When we were out playing there was a mother home in every house. That's missing today. That was a comfortable feeling. We didn't realize it at the time, but it was there and you knew it. Anything came up, all you had to do was run to one of the houses. The mothers were all at home. It didn't matter at all which house you ran to. Everybody knew everybody and pretty much all got along.

It's something you can't do with the economy today. It just doesn't happen. In the average family the mother has to work; they have no choice. But I think that had a lot to do with the feeling of community in Staatsburg, too. The mothers were always there. Monday they washed. Tuesday they did the ironing. Wednesday they baked. There was a whole routine and they never deviated. That was it. They all were doing the same thing on the same day.

You know I was thinking the other night. When we were kids, especially down on the street where Jackie Dugliss and I and the Radcliffes lived, each mother had a whistle. When it was time to come in, they'd blow the whistle, and each one had a different tone so the kid would know automatically when it was time to come home. In the fall if we didn't hear the whistle go, we knew that as soon as the streetlights came on it was time to go home.

I think the biggest thing I'd like to remember about Staatsburg was the people and how they looked out for each other. Staatsburg was a good place to be, and it still is. I think it still is. We have our problems, but I don't think there is anything that can't be worked out eventually.

March 1987
John Van Dyke

John Van Dyke is a strong, enthusiastic person who appears to be at least ten years younger than his eighty-three years. Although he currently lives in Hyde Park, he was brought up in Staatsburg where his father worked on the Langdon Estate around the turn of the century. When he was old enough, John began working on the Mills Estate, and he continued to work very hard all his life in various capacities around the town of Hyde Park.

Although we had never met before the taped interview, Mr. Van Dyke was most eager to tell me about what it was like to be employed on one of the large estates. His observations and anecdotes about the Mills family and their opulent lifestyle were given to me in a delightful, straight-forward manner.

Mr. Van Dyke's recall is astounding. Not only could he remember many details about his own youth, but he also was able to remember information that had been given to him by his grandfather. Therefore, I was able to learn some things about Staatsburg that reach back to the early mid-1800s.

Although he did not express any strong sense of nostalgia for the village of Staatsburg, Mr. Van Dyke was an excellent spokesperson for the many hard-working residents of the village who served the wealthy families on the estates.

> "Such hath it been – shall be – beneath the sun.
> The many still must labor for the one."
> –Lord Byron

I was born on May 19, 1904, and when I was seven years old we moved to a little house on Route 9. It is right across from where the Cozy Inn used to be and right next to where the nursing home is now. There was no electricity, no running water, and no toilet. We paid $4 a month until World War I and then we paid five dollars. I had electricity put in there in 1931 or 1932, but that same year they gave the place to the state and we had to move out.

We moved there because my father had a job as a farmer on the Langdon Estate. Francis G. Langdon owned all that property that is now the Anderson School. He had a lot of buildings that have burned down. There was a coach house down by the pond. The house the Langdons lived in is on a hill by the river and is part of the Anderson School. The Langdons were millionaires.

Even though my father worked on the Langdon Estate, the house we lived in was part of the Thompson Estate. The Thompson property went from where the school is now up along Old Post Road to the Langdon land and it went all back in where the Norrie State Park is now. We lived in a tenant house and there were two others that belonged to the Thompsons. One was right down where the Norrie Boat Basin is now. It was a small house just like the one I lived in. And the other was behind the big house. The big house was located on Route 9 just as you come into the village; it was on the left where the fitness course is now.

I went to the old wooden school in Staatsburg. That was quite a school years ago. They had a boys' and a girls' side to play on. And they had outhouses; one for the men and one for the women. That was a long time ago!! The school only went to the eighth grade then. I remember Miss Baldwin, Miss Turner, and Miss Culver. They were quite old when we were little kids...they're long gone now.

My father died when he was forty-nine years old. I was fifteen so I had to get going and help out. I'd do anything to make a dollar, you know. Work here, work there, do a lot of jobs around the neighborhood—didn't care where. At that time work wasn't too plentiful. I had a wood business—cut and sold wood with a little truck. I went to work on the Mills Estate and stayed there for seven years. I worked raising chickens. We used to raise 10,000 chickens a year up there. That was about 1925. We used to kill a couple of hundred chickens a week for the big house. They had lots of parties. You know, millionaires only eat the breast and throw the rest of the chicken out.

The chicken farm was across from the entrance to the Mills Estate. In the summer we used to raise the young chickens way up on the hill on the other end of the farm. The other side of Old Post Road, where the mansion is, was called the "garden side." There were greenhouses and the coach house over there. And where I worked was called the "farm side." We used to take chickens and milk from the dairy up to the big house. Believe it or not, they had morning milk with cream this thick on it, and then in the afternoon they'd pour that right down the drain and get afternoon cream! Those chefs—they didn't care for nothing!

Mrs. Mills used to complain—now the butler told me this—to Mr. Mills: "Oh, the chefs, they throw pounds of butter into the fire to make it burn more, and they waste more stuff." Well, old Ogden says, "I'll tell you. You get rid of them and get some others, they'd be just the same, and after all, we can't spend the interest on all our money." And that's true 'cause he was worth 400 million dollars when he died. That's a lot of money.

Mr. Mills, if she didn't have a cigar at her dinner plate after she ate, somebody would get hell. She was a cigar smoker—I'm going way back now.

I knew the butler very well and he was a millionaire butler. Tompkins, his name was—he became a millionaire working for Mills. When World War I was on, Mills offered him I don't know how many thousands of dollars to go to Europe because the family owned a whole village or city over there, and they were worried about it during the war. So Mills offered the butler a big amount of money if he'd go over with him. Tompkins did, and of course he became a millionaire.

Sometimes you'd have to contact Mr. Mills about something on the farm. I used to do the buying for all the poultry on the chicken farm. When Mills was going up and down the paths of the estate, if he was swinging that cane you could get anything off of him you wanted, but if he was just pounding the cane straight up and down—stay away from him—he was on the warpath! I never asked that man for anything that he didn't say go ahead and get it. Like I'd need thousands of gallons of kerosene to spray the chicken coops to keep the lice off them. "Get whatever you want; get whatever you want!" That was the answer. I had a pretty good job there.

Mr. Mills couldn't have been any better to his employees. The family used to have these big parties up to the big house. Of course there were a lot of poor people around the village and Mr. Mills let them come in on a Monday or after a holiday and pick over the chicken parts that weren't used at the party. Well, always someone has to spoil it. They got to fighting out there one day because someone got two more chickens than someone else, and old man Mills heard it. "Stop it; stop it," he said. "Let 'em go to the meat market and get all the meat they want; I'll pay the bill. I don't want no more of this monkey business." That's just the way he was.

He gave Vassar Hospital and St. Francis Hospital an ambulance every year, but he wanted no publicity whatsoever. That's the kind of man he was. He didn't want nobody to know nothing about what he did, see.

He used to do a lot for the people, I'm telling you. There was a hobo used to go North. Every single summer he'd stop to see Mr. Mills. He'd get a twenty dollar bill—that was big money years ago—and when he went back in the fall, he'd stop and Mr. Mills would give him another twenty. He was very good hearted. We used to get our coal, believe it or not, delivered in our basements for four dollars a ton. Kidder Coal Company would bring it right in...Mr. Mills was a great guy.

And Mrs. Mills. She used to go over through Mills Cross Road and Reservoir Road sometimes. This lady lived there. Her name was Rowe and her husband worked on the garden side of the Mill's Estate. And she was out there dragging water out of the well, putting it in these old buckets. You know how they used to years ago—bring water back and forth to scrub laundry and stuff. Well, Mrs. Mills happened to go by there one day and she said, "My good woman, what are you doing?"

"Oh, I'm getting water up here to do my wash. I have to cart the water."

Mrs. Mills said, "Don't you cart no more water. I'll have a plumber come in here and I'll have your house hooked right up to water." That was Mrs. Mills. They were big-hearted people, you see.

The Mills went to St. Margaret's Church, but they didn't go into the village for anything else. Someone else did all the shopping for them. They would come up from the city by limousine—great big cars with chauffeurs. In the summer they spent a lot of time here—big parties, play golf—the sky was the limit in those days. The coachman would bring them down from the big house to the golf course in a special horse and carriage. They'd play golf most every day. I used to caddy for Mrs. Mills when I was a kid.

She'd pick me up at school and bring me to the course. She couldn't hit a golf ball from here to across the street, but she thought she could. Then I'd have to get the ball and bring it back for her. She used to pay fifty cents a hour. I figured that was pretty good money at that time. Old Man Mills would always give the kids a dollar a round, and if there weren't enough guests that needed caddies, he'd still pay the kids a dollar and let them sit on the fence and watch. He wanted to take care of everybody.

The Mills did a lot of good for the people in Staatsburg—a lot of good. Everything they wanted, they had. On the chicken farm, we were entitled to all the eggs and chicken and turkey we wanted. We used to get eggs by the water pail and snowball each other because we had so many eggs we didn't know what to do with them all.

We always had chicken at home—every week, every week. A neighbor of ours used to give us ham and we'd give him chicken. He was tickled to death and we were so sick and tired of chicken, we were tickled to death with the ham. We always had plenty to eat.

The seven years I worked there I killed 23,000 fowls. That's a lot of fowl. They'd ship them to the city for parties, sometimes. They'd have two or three hundred for a party up here and then they'd go down to Long Island or New York where the other place was and have another big party. The feed bill on the chicken part of the farm alone—you wouldn't believe it—16,000 dollars! My God with all those chickens you'd have to bring in a lot of feed, and they'd give them the best stuff there was. We used to get the cod liver oil in a fifty-gallon drum. 'Course that was very expensive. Then we used to get this prepared buttermilk to feed them. They got the best food they could get and it kept those chickens in good shape.

We used to take the chickens to the Dutchess County Fair and the Danbury Fair to show them. Mills would pay all the entry fees and we got to keep all the premiums the chickens won. Oh, we used to get sometimes five or six hundred dollars up at the fairgrounds. The farmers couldn't compete with Mills. But, whatever we made, we got to split it up between us.

On the farm at one time, Mills had sheep and pigs. They also had two sets of Belgian horses that weighed sixteen or seventeen [hundred] pounds apiece. And you know they had the best cows in the country. They had a grand champion of the world—"Civil Service" they called her. She was a grand champion. They used to pay $60,000 apiece for young heifers. That cow barn was all white tile where the cows stayed. Electric fans; heat in the wintertime; oh boy, it was better than some people's houses. They had their own dairy right there. Made their own butter, and they were always testing the cows' milk—that was some rich milk, too.

The Depression was bad for a lot of people in Staatsburg. They really depended on the estates to help out a little bit, then. There was a lot of work there. They didn't get big money—good Lord, I know when I worked with the chickens I got $60 a month. Some people just tried to get along as best they could during the Depression.

I worked on the Mills Estate for seven years and then I got a job on the New York Central Railroad as a carpenter. At one time I worked part time for the Hoyt Estate, too. Mr. and Mrs. Gerald Hoyt; Lydig Hoyt was the son. He and his wife came in later. She was an actress, I think. Lydig was a nice fella, but I knew the old man a little better.

When I was a kid I was walking up the road by the old schoolhouse. Gerald Hoyt always used to be taking a hike. Well, you know kids mosey—I came trotting right up next to him. He wanted to know what my name was and this, that, and the other thing. I told him, and he gave me a quarter. Then he asked me, "What are you gonna do with that quarter?"

"Oh, I'm gonna take it and put it in the bank, or maybe I'll buy myself a necktie."

He said, "You put it in the bank and I'll send you some neckties."

My God, he sent me a box of neckties. I'm telling you there were enough neckties to go from here to the end of the street! They were knitted ties, too. I had quite a job tying them. But he did that. He said, "Put that quarter in the bank and I'll send you neckties."

The Hoyt Estate had three greenhouses and I had to keep them fired at night all winter long. They had one special greenhouse just to grow mushrooms. They had gardens to supply the house with flowers. In wintertime they took ice in off the river and put it in icehouses so they would have ice all summer long; that was before refrigeration. The Hoyts were rich people; they had parties, too, but they didn't go overboard like Mills.

I'll go right along now, and just tell you what I know about Staatsburg and what was told to me. My grandfather told me all about a lot of this. He was born in Clinton, but lived around here for many years.

The Whitehead Sand Company was just south of where Stone's Farm was on Route 9. They had barges come into the big docks down on the river, and they would load them up with sand and take them into New York City.

Right across from Stone's Farm there used to be a great big blue barn. That was one of the places where the stagecoaches used to change their horses going from New York City to Albany. That was before my time.

Then we come north to where the Hyde Park Nursing Home is now. There used to be a fish market where the nursing home sets now. That was operated by Barton Hover. North of that was a fish hook factory. They made fish hooks large enough so you could catch a shark, and that was operated by Gardner Merritt. The building is all torn down now. It was between the nursing home and that next house north.

Then you go from there and come north to the Enderkill Creek on Old Post Road as you come into the village. That used to be part of the Thompson property years ago. Well, my grandfather used to say they had mules pull barges up that creek to the bridges near where the school is now. The farmers would come with their horse and wagons and pick up the feed and grain and stuff that the barges would unload. That creek was all cut out years ago—the barges would come right up to that bridge.

Go north to the four corners. The brick building on one corner is where Sam's Plumbing Shop used to be, and behind that Whites used to run a big greenhouse there years ago. That's all long torn down, now.

Jimmy Horan had a saloon on the corner across from the plumbing store. Next to that was Bodenstein's Ice Tool Factory. Across from that was a blacksmith shop, run by Charlie Wilbert. Now that I do just remember.

Across the railroad tracks there used to be a creamery. Farmers would bring milk and they'd ship it into New York. After that came Overton's. He had a factory in there. He used to make marlin spikes, scrapers, spades, and shovels. Ships used marlin spikes for splicing cables. Across the way was Kidder Coal Company, but they moved later on.

Down River Road was the Staatsburg dock. Boats used to stop there and leave freight and passengers off. South of that were two huge icehouses owned by Knickerbocker Ice Company. They used to harvest the ice in the wintertime and ship it to New York City in the summertime. Refrigeration wasn't thought of in those days. East of where the railroad station was there was a huge grocery store owned by Ernest Bodenstein. I can just remember that, but I was pretty

small then. Across from that was a shoemaker shop run by Mike Profirio. South of that was the barber shop operated by Fred Hess.

Then you go north up Railroad Avenue. There was a butcher shop—Schouten's—and there was Hughes's Store. At the end of the street, near the tracks, Bromheads used to have a saloon there. Kidder took that over for the coal company later on. Just south of that, which is long gone now, was a shed. Staatsburg Fire Company had a little truck in there they pulled by hand, and they had little buckets on the side. That was a long, long time ago. My grandfather told me about that. Then come to the end of West Elm Avenue and on that corner there used to be an ice cream parlor.

Johnny Millard had an ice cream parlor, too, across from the Methodist Church on Market Street. East of that was Parker Plumbing. Broadfield had a saloon across from where the post office is now, on the corner of Market Street. They had a lot of drinking places in Staatsburg, didn't they?

Go back to Mulford Avenue, now. Across from the Catholic Church was a town hall. They had dances and movies, but it burned down eventually. I used to see "Voice on the Wire" and all those old timers years and years ago. They had a lot of dances—masquerades, they used to have there. Next to that was a little garage; the first automobile garage ever put in Staatsburg. Run by Walter Hagadorn. Long gone now. A little further up on the left side of the street was a bicycle shop.

Dr. Herridon lived on Mulford Avenue, and he was our family doctor. He had been my mother's doctor for years. Dr. Herridon was a great man for setting bones. I fell off a roof one time—25 feet and landed on my feet. Broke one ankle; sprained the other. Dr. Herridon fixed it perfect. I was lucky I landed on my feet on the soft ground. A friend put me in his car and took me right down to the doctor.

He made house calls—too many sometimes. He'd keep right on coming, even after you were well. It cost probably only a dollar or a dollar and a half, but that was a lot of money for some people. You'd have to tell him to stop coming!

Staatsburg used to be nothing but swamp, you know. My grandfather used to say the only way they could get hay was to get on the bogs and cut the hay here and there in the summertime. The bogs and swamps used to come up, you know. There's a lot of quicksand, too. They lost part of the school when they were building it because of quicksand.

At one time nothing would travel on the road from Hyde Park to Staatsburg for two days when there was snow. We used to ski on it. Then a farmer would take out a horse and cutter and sleigh and break it open. But we used to go back and forth to school on our skis; it was the only way we could get there.

We used to ice skate a lot. Langdon's Pond was a great place to skate. Bill White, who was Sam White's son, used to take care of all us kids. He'd make sure we got our skates on and see that the straps were right. And they had a big pavilion there with a great big fireplace in it that's all torn down now. We'd take potatoes in there and cook them. Oh, we had a ball skating. Bill took care of all us kids and then he got into World War I and went over there and got killed.

The Norrie family lived at the Morgan's place. It was over River Road on the right somewhere; it's all torn down. I knew Lewis Norrie when we were just kids. We all played together. The family was just up for the summertime, but he'd go swimming down at the river with us. And he was a good skater, too. He'd come around and take the kids for a ride in his car, this and that. Millionaires, you know, they have everything. We were really living it up with him. Poor guy cracked up and got killed in his car. That's why that memorial is there in the park. He was quite a guy.

Of course in those days the Hudson River wasn't quite as dirty as it was in later years. My grandfather could remember standing at the lower part of Main Street in Poughkeepsie, where the dock used to be and looking down and seeing the bottom of the Hudson River.

In Staatsburg, George Ackert and I are the only ones left who ever worked on the Mills Estate. Everyone else is dead and gone. We also used to shovel coal together for Kidder. When we delivered coal and lumber for Kidder, we got $3 a day for nine hours of work. That was big money.

Any of the estates were good to work for. Of course Dinsmore and Huntington or Hoyt did not pay as much as Mills. The Mills and the Vanderbilts paid more than anyone, but I guess they had more money than the rest of them. Langdon's, where my father worked, they were rich, but not like the Mills. But they did pretty well with their help. My father used to get all his wood, vegetables, and milk there. That was a big help.

Every Christmas Langdons had a Christmas tree at the big house and they had all the help that worked on the estate come there. They had a list of two things you wanted. If you didn't get one, you got the other. Every Christmas, everyone who worked there and their kids got a present.

Mr. Mills used to give kids a nickel for every dandelion they could pull out of the lawn up there in the spring of the year. He used to get ten or fifteen kids around the village who could use the money—five cents for every dandelion they could dig out. That was nothing to him.

Mr. and Mrs. Mills liked to take walks every day. He never missed much. He'd go around the look the place over. He was quite a guy. When that old cane was swinging, boy, you could get anything, but when it was banging like this—stay away from him!

1983

Naomi Craft

I met with Mrs. Craft in her house on Mulford Avenue on a very warm summer day in 1983. She had been widowed in 1967 and lived alone since that time. Just prior to my visit, Mrs. Craft had suffered a hip injury which kept her confined to a chair and a walker.

Although she was shy at first, Mrs. Craft soon warmed to the topic of her childhood in Staatsburg and proved to have an excellent memory for details.

Naomi Craft was a tiny woman with a hearty, infectious giggle. Throughout the interview, a child-like enthusiasm emerged in her eagerness to share fond memories.

"I have had playmates, I have had companions.
In my days of childhood, in my joyful school days…"
–Charles Lamb, 1798

MY FATHER, WILLIAM FRICKER, was brought up in the gardening business. His father came from England and was the head of some greenhouses in the city of Poughkeepsie, and for thirty-two years my father lived in the Glebe House. He was about nineteen years old during the blizzard of '88 and he told me they lost a lot of glass from that terrible storm. Those greenhouses are all torn down now.

My family first came to Staatsburg in 1906 when I was six years old. We had come from Newport, Rhode Island, where my father had worked on a large estate. But that estate closed down so he came here to be a gardener for the Dinsmores. We lived in the big stone house on the Old Post Road. That was a two-family tenant house of the Dinsmores. A very old couple named Whalen lived in the other side of the house. He worked for Mr. Dinsmore, too. The stone house is much nicer now than when we lived there.

I remember we had peddlers who came to the door. My mother used to buy tea from Atlantic & Pacific—A & P. They'd come up with a horse and wagon. There were also fruit peddlers, beer wagons, and a butcher from Hyde Park came up and sold meat.

When we moved to Staatsburg, my father worked in the Dinsmore greenhouse in the winter. He grew orchids, roses, and carnations. I gave a picture of my father outside the greenhouse to Ned Leadbitter. In the summer he worked in their "Grandmother's Garden." Every day I would bring him his lunch. I would walk all the way from the stone house to the Dinsmore Estate. We would take our lunch on the riverbank, then take a rowboat ride during his noon hour break. I would walk him home after work. My father spoiled me; I was an only child and an only grandchild so I guess I was a little spoiled.

I went to the wooden schoolhouse which was next to where the brick school is now. In those days there were two classes in each room, but I don't think we used the upstairs for anything. My best friend, Bea White, brought me to school on the first day. I always wore ribbons in my hair. My aunt used to work in a florist shop and send me pretty ribbons—maybe that's why.

I think we learned about the same things you kids learn today—reading, writing, and arithmetic. We had to work very hard. I remember one time the principal, Mr. Hicks, said to us, "I bet you people don't even know how to add." Then he made us stay until 6 o'clock at night adding up long columns of numbers for him at the blackboard with a pointer stick. My father had already come home from work when I got home from school that night. But, I will tell you one thing, I sure did learn to add after that! The schools were very strict, but you learned a lot.

Our teachers were Miss Ovitt and Miss Simmons. I loved Miss Ovitt. She was so nice. I liked Miss Simmons, too. She was very strict, but I think I was her pet. At recess we played jump rope and tisket-a-tasket—simple games like that.

The boys were not allowed to come over on the side of the playground with the girls. There was a big fence up to separate us. I don't know why they did that. You know we had outdoor plumbing in those days in that old school. We had to go outside in the cold. Boy, I almost froze! I don't think we went to the bathroom too often.

In the winter I wasn't allowed to go out much after school to play because it got dark. But at school we used to have a big sleigh ride. I guess it was the Dinsmores or the Mills used to have one of the men come and take us in a big horse-drawn sleigh up to Rhinebeck.

I'd freeze to death, but it sure was fun. We used to have a pond—Langdon's Pond. I didn't go skating, but my father was a wonderful skater. Mostly in the winter, though, I'd study. I had a lot of studying to do.

There was no Community Day when I was a kid, but we did have parades, and on Saturdays there were ball games down at the ballfield. They had grandstands there. St. Margaret's Church used to have family picnics across the river somewhere—West Point, I think. And, we used to go to Mills Cove where there was a beach and you could take picnics. I was never allowed to go there alone when I was young because I couldn't swim. When we still lived in Newport, and I was about five or six, my father said he learned to swim when somebody threw him in. Well, he did that to me and it was the wrong thing because I panicked and I never would learn. If I got in the water I would just panic. My father was a wonderful swimmer, and he thought I could learn, but I'm not one you can push into things.

When we got older, we had to go to school in Poughkeepsie because the Staatsburg School only went to tenth grade. From there we would finish high school at the school that is now Our Lady of Lourdes. Then it was the Poughkeepsie High School. I still remember we took the 7:22 train in the morning and came home at 5:22. There were about six or seven girls who all went together. Let me see, there was Bea White, Catherine Hayes, Geraldine Brogley (her name is Smith now), and May Emerson, and me. There were two boys who weren't really in our class—Dick Harmon and Bill Blair. Oh, and Anna Kilmer and Sara Kilmer. Angie Gick wasn't from Staatsburg; she used to get the train further up in Red Hook, I think. From the Poughkeepsie station we would walk up to South Hamilton Street to the school. Even though it was a long day, we sure had a lot of fun on that train.

The railroad station in Staatsburg was new when we went to high school. It was very nice. The rich people would come on the weekends and the coachman would pick them up at the station. It was a busy place in those days. There weren't many cars back then. My father never had a car. We always took trains or buses. Buses used to go right through the middle of town. One came from Red Hook and it was an open bus with long benches going down each side. Now there's no transportation in Staatsburg.

After high school, some of my friends went to college to become teachers. Some of them went to work on the estates. I went to the Eastman School in Poughkeepsie for a six-month business course. The first job I got was at the Mitchell Furniture Store. I didn't like it there because the lady told me I had to sell things to people. She told me to tell them how nice they looked. I couldn't tell people they looked nice if they didn't! The man who was the boss liked me; he said I did good work. He was so nice, but I didn't like this girl.

The men used to kid me. I was so bashful, you know, and they used to tell me I had to work late. I would get upset and tell them I couldn't stay late because I couldn't go down to that station by myself at night. They would only be fooling me. I didn't have the nerve to quit, so finally my father wrote a note saying I wasn't coming to work there any more. You see, before that I had met Mr. Kidder, and he asked me to come to work for him. He owned the coal yard in Staatsburg. I became the very first office girl at Kidder Coal. I did bookkeeping and shorthand. I used to weigh a good lot of tons of coal because the Mills and Dinsmores used to get coal for their help. They had a scale and I'd weigh it. Then it would go to the people and Mills and Dinsmore would pay for it. I liked it there because it was very close to home. My mother and I had moved to a house on Railroad Avenue after my father died. It was owned by Mr. Kidder and it was close to my office so I could walk to work.

When I got married, I stopped working. Once in awhile I helped out when they were busy, like with income tax and things. My husband and I got free coal from Kidder's—it came with the job! Kidder's Coal went out of business after oil came in. Coal wasn't needed and the business went on the blink.

I met my husband when I worked in the office. He always came in to buy things, and one time he asked me for a date. I had always liked him, but I never let on! We went to the county fair on our first date. We married in 1928 and lived on the South Cross Road. That was during the Depression and it was hard, but we lived on a farm our first year so we had plenty to eat—not much money, but plenty of food. We've seen hard times. The kids today don't know what it is.

Staatsburg was a nice little village then. There were lots of stores and businesses. Across from Osterhoudt's store there was a meat market, and the post office used to be in Osterhoudt's. There was an ice cream store, a plumbing store, and another grocery store. We had an ice tool factory, and icehouses on the river. There was a great big hotel across from Leadbitter's, and several more big hotels. Mrs. Bodenstein lived in that lovely house across from the railroad station. Across from the station there was another store and a barber shop. The station is gone now, but the building that was the barber store is still next to the tracks.

Of course, we had Dr. Herridon on Mulford Avenue. I usually went to Dr. Cronk, though, in Hyde Park. I remember one time when we were going to Poughkeepsie High School, they had the epidemic of polio. That was in 1917. A girl that went to school with us died of it. We were quarantined for a week. They wouldn't let us in the high school. They had a lot more of it in Poughkeepsie, but even so they wouldn't let the kids from Staatsburg in. Well, anyway, we had to go to the doctor's for an examination before we could go back to school. Down in Newport you couldn't get into school unless you were vaccinated. I had never been. My dad didn't want me to, but my mother made him so I could get into school. Mine never took—there was no mark. When my mother took me back to the doctor, he said I was immune.

I remember the town hall on Mulford Avenue. The building has been torn down. We had dances and minstrel shows with local talent. There was another store across from St. Margaret's Church on Old Post Road. The main road used to go right through the village. The town didn't seem to prosper so much when they built the new road.

Oh, it was so nice. Everybody kept the houses so nice—lawns and flowers. It doesn't look like that anymore.

(Mrs. Craft passed away in January of 1986.)

March 1987

Edith Kidder

I met Mrs. Edith Kidder through a mutual friend and former Staatsburg resident, Grace Traver. On an unseasonably warm Sunday in March, Grace took me to the Ferncliff Nursing Home in Rhinebeck where Mrs. Kidder welcomed us to her room.

Before our interview, Grace and Mrs. Kidder exchanged news about family and friends, while I observed this impressive lady of ninety-nine years. She is a robust woman with a delightful laugh and an extremely positive attitude. A lovely painting of the Kidder family home on Old Post Road hung in a prominent place in her room, and Mrs. Kidder explained proudly that it had been painted by her son. From the window of her room, she has a beautiful view, and Mrs. Kidder commented on how pleasant it is to watch the seasons change on the mountains.

As we talked, I learned not only about the village of Staatsburg, but also about a long-past era of gracious living in a town and a world that moved at a much gentler pace than it does today.

Perhaps one of the secrets to Mrs. Kidder's longevity is her interest in the people and the place where she lived for many years. As I asked her questions about the Staatsburg of yesterday, Mrs. Kidder asked me almost as many questions about the village as it is today.

> "Where the quiet-colored end of evening smiles…"
> –Robert Browning

I was born in 1888 up in Martinsburg, almost up to the Canadian line. My mother died so I went with my aunt and uncle and was brought up in Flushing, Long Island. I lived there for about eighteen years.

We used to go back up to Martinsburg in the summer. My father had kept the house up there and he'd open it up in the summertime. I met my husband there. He came up with Elizabeth Champlin from Staatsburg. Her husband and George were cousins and she brought George up one summer and that's how I met him.

I came to Staatsburg in 1911 when I was married. After about a year we bought the house on Old Post Road. The house was the original Mulford farmhouse, and three or four different families owned it after that. We bought it from Mrs. Arnold. The Markle house on Mulford Avenue was a tenant house for the farm at one time.

Our house had about eight rooms and a room in the attic that we never used. There were three fireplaces—one in the living room, one in the bedroom upstairs, and a nice big one in the kitchen. It was an old-fashioned kitchen. I suppose at one time they used the fireplaces to heat the house. We put the furnace in when we moved there. The house used to have a big front porch, too.

We had a lovely big garden in our backyard—grew potatoes and a lot of things. We only grew one side of the yard and that was plenty of room. We had corn, lima beans.

We had chickens at one time. We had a goat at one time, and we had a rabbit at one time! All the things that little boys like—cats and dogs and everything. When we first moved there we had a horse.

We went to Poughkeepsie in a horse and carriage, and a couple of times we went in the winter by horse-drawn sleigh. We bundled up good and it was just nice. It took a whole hour to get to Poughkeepsie that way. We had a barn and an open lot down below where we kept the horse in the summertime. We tore the barn down and built a garage after we got a car. I don't remember whatever happened to the horse.

There used to be a lot of traffic when Old Post Road was a main road through Staatsburg. The boys—Nels and Fred—used to sit on the front porch and count the cars go by on the weekends. There'd be a bunch of them; there were a lot of cars. The road used to be halfway up our front lawn. About 1911 or 1912, a little after we got the house, they changed the road and put it down where it is now, so we got quite a lot of front yard there.

I think the village looked a lot nicer when I first came than it does now. Millards lived right next to us, and then came Arnold's house. Everyone kept their homes so nice. We had a nice sidewalk out in front. Are there any sidewalks still there? Ours disappeared when the milk trucks came because they'd ride right up on them.

I used to trade at Borner's Store and usually we'd go once a week to Poughkeepsie to one of the big grocery stores down there, or we'd go to Rhinebeck. We went by car. Ed Hughes owned the store when we were there. He was Mrs. Barker's brother—she was a Hughes.

There was a meat market in the village and another grocery store—that was Leo's and Seamans bought it after that. Then at one time there was Mr. Millard's store. That was an ice cream parlor. Maggie Justus lives there now.

Across from the library there was a little store on the corner of Elm Street that goes down near where our office used to be. The Cashins lived down that street. On the corner across from that store was the house where Wiseman's lived. The Deans live there now.

To buy clothes we went to Poughkeepsie. Luckey Platts and Wallaces were both lovely department stores. We bought the boys things at Schwartz's—that was a good store. When we first moved to Staatsburg, we'd take the train in to Poughkeepsie quite often. From the station we'd take the trolley up Main Street to the stores and restaurant, and the French Pastry up past Luckey's was very good, also.

The Kidder Coal office in Staatsburg was first down below the train station where Freddie Hess later had his barbershop. We built that for our office and the coal pocket was across the tracks from that. Naomi Craft was the first office girl there and she worked for us for many years. Eleanor Burke worked in the office, too. Then we bought Bromheads Hotel at the end of Elm Street and put our offices there. The coal pockets and all were in the back of that. I don't remember what year that was.

Parker's shop was a plumbing store up near Leo's on Market Street. Then Sam White got his plumbing store on the corner of Mulford Avenue and he had the plumbing business in town.

I remember when Bodenstein's Tool Shop burned. We watched it because it was windy and all the sparks blew over our way, and we had a shingled roof! That was quite a big fire.

There were two hotels in the village when we first moved in. Down at the end of one street was Bromheads, and the other one was on Old Post Road across from the post office where that empty lot is now. I think it was Grace Bodenstein's people who owned that one—Broadfield? It was a big hotel, but it wasn't there very long after I was there. I think they tore it down. The Bromhead—we bought that and it was our office, but the other one was torn down.

Is the stone pile on that vacant lot still there? They put stones there—Mr. Barker and somebody else—and they wanted to build a bank in Staatsburg. But they couldn't get enough others interested. They brought those stones down from a farmer's up on the hill.

My boys went to the old wooden school at first. It was a good school to start with until they built the new one.

In the winter the kids went skating. Sometimes they'd go up on the reservoir. They never went sledding on the Mills property in those days; they never went over there.

In the summer the kids played ball and they used to go down to Norrie Park to swim when they were older. Fred had a boat and he would go down on the river. It was nice down there then. All the kids went down. Is anything left down there now? There were two houses right near the park—Bart Hinds's and the other one was Gillespie's. Quite a nice big house—they tore that one down. Did they tear down Hinds's?

The town hall was owned by Tony Leo and he showed movies there. Dorothy Nichols played the piano. I don't think it was there very long. I only went a few times.

We had a card club with twelve of us and we'd meet once a week to play Bridge. Sometimes two or three of the teachers would join it. We went to a different house every week. 'Course the teachers couldn't have us—they were boarding—but the rest of us would take turns each week. Let's see, some of the women who joined were Mrs. Arnold—Adelaide; Mrs. Seaman; Mrs. Stevenson; Miss Gallagher and Miss Keyes were teachers; and Gladys Hennion. Her house was down by Norrie Point entrance—that's all torn down.

The churches were all active. They used to have a table at Community Day to sell things. I heard the Methodist Church was bought by a woman and it looks lovely now.

A lot of people in Staatsburg worked on the estates. They were opened up and busy when I first lived there. They made quite a lot of work for the townspeople in those days. You would see the people who lived on the estates once in a while. We used to see Mrs. Hoyt

more than anyone else; she did a lot in the village. The Hoyt House was lovely. I hope they try to save that one—it was a shame to let it run down. When the estates closed, they took away a lot of business. They were big customers. They all traded in Staatsburg.

I went to Dr. Herridon and I knew Mrs. Herridon very well. We were friends and used to go around together—we'd take little trips. Sometimes a bunch of us would go over to Lake Mohonk for the day and Mrs. Herridon would come along. They had two daughters—Edna and Mildred. Later on I went to Dr. Cronk. He was from Hyde Park, but he would come up to Staatsburg every day if you needed him.

Grace Bodenstein and I watched for airplanes during World War II. We went to the tower in the afternoons. Usually it was a two-hour watch, but it went on for twenty-four hours a day.

I remember when World War I ended. At the firehouse there was a meeting of ladies who did Red Cross work and things like that. In those days, instead of a fire whistle they had a big, round metal thing they used to hammer. Well, the ladies came out of the meeting and they took the hammer—Mrs. Huntington and all of them—and they hammered it good when the war ended!

I came to Staatsburg in 1911 and I lived there about fifty years. It was a nice place to live. It was quiet. I had a lot of nice friends, and that's about it.

March 1987

Kenneth Stewart

Ken Stewart is a name that is familiar to many people in the Staatsburg area. Having worked as a teacher and then a principal in the village school for a total of thirty-seven years, Mr. Stewart had a strong influence on the education of most of the local children.

He was very willing to come to Staatsburg from his home in Rhinebeck for our interview, and for a man eighty-four years old, I found Mr. Stewart to have an uncanny memory for details about specific people, dates, and events regarding the village.

Although he has been retired since 1971, Mr. Stewart was most eager to talk about education as it is today as well as what it was like when he began teaching. He remains very well informed about local school systems and community affairs.

For those of you who knew Mr. Stewart as your teacher, coach, principal, or colleague, you will be interested to learn that he is still a man of very strong opinions, who tends to view things as either black or white. He still conducts himself with great dignity and self-assurance. And he probably remembers more about your childhood than you would ever possibly believe!

"Education is...hanging around until you've caught on."
–Robert Frost

I FIRST CAME TO STAATSBURG SCHOOL in 1933 to teach business courses, physical education, and to coach. I had graduated from NYU in 1927 with a bachelor of commercial science degree, and was working in New York on Wall Street in a brokerage house when the market crashed. When I started, there were 1,300 employees and when they let me go there were only 600 left. They called me a week or so later and wanted me to come back to work, but they said there was no guarantee of how long they could keep me. I said, "You don't want me." Meantime, I had gone back to NYU to get a science degree so I could coach and teach.

While I was taking a course at NYU, I heard about the job at Staatsburg through a teachers' agency. I came up to see Harry Barker, the president of the school board. He was a lawyer in Poughkeepsie and he was the one who built the school up here—Harry Barker, quite a character. I came up to his office in Poughkeepsie and we talked for awhile when he said, "Well, we'll go up home." So he called his chauffeur and we rode up to his house in Staatsburg. It's the house where the Aldens live now.

We sat in Harry Barker's library and he wanted to know if I wanted a cigarette. I said, "No, Mr. Barker, I don't smoke." Would I have a cocktail? "No, Mr. Barker, I don't drink." So he called his wife and she brought him a cocktail which he sat and drank. Then he said, "You're going to stay for dinner." Just like that! "You're going to stay for dinner." So I did, and then he wanted me to take a ride around and speak with the school board members. He called Walt Cronk, who was the school board's attorney, and I got into Walt's car and went out to see Phil Cookingham and Harry Traver. When we got back, Harry Barker said, "What do you think? Are you interested in the job?" I said I thought I was. He said, "Well, it's yours." And I was hired. Nobody ever said anything then, but I think if I had taken that

drink or that cigarette, I would not have gotten the job. That's the way it was done down here then.

I got the job through Harry Barker, and the next night I was in that class at NYU and I got talking to a fellow in the course. He wanted to know what I was doing and I told him I had just gotten a job up in Staatsburg. He said, "I'm principal of the school in Staatsburg!" That was Baker. Irwin Baker was the principal, but Harry Barker fired and hired. He was "IT." People said he had a white elephant when he built this school. He said he'd have the Hyde Park students up here, but people didn't believe him. And he did get them up here. But it was a white elephant people said, building that big school in Staatsburg.

Hyde Park and Staatsburg each had two-year high schools until Staatsburg built the new building here. Then all the Hyde Park kids came up here to finish school. When I first came as coach, the principal, Baker, called me aside and said, "You know, I think you might have some trouble with your basketball team. Half of these kids will be from Hyde Park, and half of them will be from Staatsburg, and these people don't like each other." I told him I wouldn't have any trouble, and I never did have a bit of trouble. I had some good ball players from Hyde Park on my teams. They all got along wonderfully together. The kids always got along in school together. It was the adults who had the problems.

I coached girls' basketball. We had a championship team and nobody around here could touch us for two or three years. Anna Sinibaldi was a tremendous basketball player. She wasn't one of those six-foot gals you see around today at Red Hook and Roosevelt, but I would still like to have my girls play one of these teams today just to show how good my team was. We played all the local teams around—Arlington, Wappingers, Red Hook. We played the big schools and we beat them all.

Then the state discontinued girls' basketball. It was too tough for the girls, they said. They couldn't play anymore!! I said girls operate the same as boys, and when they were playing basketball they weren't out running around and carousing around! They were going home tired after practice and they didn't have a chance to run around. Well, we would have had a good team in the next few years, too, but the state wouldn't let us have one. This was in 1934, 35. We had a good bunch of gals.

Anna was a better basketball player than most of the boys I had. She was a nice girl. She was so down-to-earth; just a good gal. They tried to induct her into the D. C. Basketball Hall of Fame. They asked me to talk to her because when they had first suggested her name, Anna said nope—she was no Hall of Famer, and she wouldn't let them put her name up. I told her, "Anna, you're better than most of these clowns that they're putting in there."

She said, "No, I didn't do anything to make a hall of fame."

And she wouldn't let them put her name in. She was quite a gal.

I was a teacher for seven years before I became principal in 1941. I taught three commercial classes, three physical education courses. I had a homeroom, supervised the playground at noontime, and I coached after school. Well, teachers taught in those days; they worked. Some character—a teacher down at Roosevelt a few years ago—said no teacher should have more than twenty-five kids in a study hall. Well, I had a study hall down here with 125 kids and another one with 90 kids and you could hear a pin drop. Forty or forty-two kids in a class was nothing.

When I came to teach in Staatsburg, I lived my first two years with Mrs. Bodenstein. I boarded—had a room upstairs. That was the big house behind the iron fence on Old Post Road. Then the next couple of years I lived with Branagans and then I got married. My wife and I lived over on Elm Avenue in a house the Barkers owned. We lived there for a couple of years but we had to move because Mrs. Barker needed it after her husband died. We looked all over Staatsburg for a house to buy but that was in the days when you couldn't find a place to live. I finally found the house in Rhinebeck, and we've been there ever since.

A couple of years later at a school board meeting, some character in town believed the principal should live in the community. I told them I lived in Rhinebeck because it was the only place I could find a home. I had tried to buy a couple of places in Staatsburg and couldn't get them. Well, this character got up at a board meeting and made a motion that principals be required to live in the community. I remember Madelline Crapser, who lived in town but taught in Poughkeepsie, got up and said she couldn't see any reason why principals had to live in the community. They took a vote and the only ones in favor of his motion were the guy who made it and the guy who seconded it; all the rest were opposed. That took care of my living out of town!

When I came to Staatsburg in 1933, there were a lot of stores. We had a meat market—Schouten's. He used to give us livers for our cat. Then Ackerman opened a store and ran it for a number of years. I remember we used to have two trains stopping both ways every day. Harry Stickle was a school board member and was the station agent here. One year my wife came up on the train for some function when she was new to the community. Well, she got off the train at the ballfield because she didn't know enough to go to the front of the train to get off. She had to walk all the way up the tracks to the station. She wondered what kind of place she was getting into, but after she moved here she never wanted to leave.

Old Post Road used to be the main road through here. They cut some of the north part of the golf course to put the highway—Route 9—through up there. One year a group of us put in some money and we ran that golf course for awhile. A fellow by the name of Shreve who lived in the stone house on Old Post Road, got us together. But I guess he found out he couldn't do it too well and he cut it out. Then it was given to the state and they fouled it up by putting the clubhouse up where it is now. The club should have been down at the stables they had at the foot of the hill—a beautiful building. They could have made some golf club there, but up where it is, when you finish the ninth or eighteenth hole, you've got to walk up a hill. It kills you! There was some talk when the state took it over that Schouten's house was going to be the clubhouse, but then they built that rock up on the hill—a terrible place.

The first couple of years I was here, probably 80% of the kids in school had parents who worked on the estates. Then it started changing over. People started moving out into other industries. A lot of these houses were built by estate owners for their employees. The people who lived next to us, the Crapsers, he worked up on the Hull Estate, I think, and he got the house through them. The Hulls, the Astors, the Dinsmores, Mills, Langdon—they're the people who built the houses in this town.

One year the Hoyts complained about the school taxes being too high. Mr. Hoyt called the school and I told him I'd come up and talk to him about it. I was the one who made out the budget so I had to know how to explain it! I went up to their house and told him how his tax rate was figured. He said, "Well, I understand it now, and I appreciate it." After that everything was all right and we became friends. Mrs. Hoyt was connected with the library in the village and every once in awhile she'd need something run off on our ditto machine, and she'd call me. We'd run them off for her at the school. We got to be pretty good friends.

The people here in Staatsburg were good about the school budget. One year they needed an oil burner, and a new bus, and something else. I figured out what each one would cost and broke it all down for the people on paper. We presented it at the annual meeting. Instead of just accepting one or two items, they finally decided to vote for everything we needed. We didn't hide anything from the people. I think that's why we got a lot of things we wanted.

One year at school we had no drinking water from September to January. We had to hire a man to get water from a well and fill up the water coolers. The kids never drank so much water in all their lives as they did for those six months! They were using 2,000 paper cups a day. The reservoir had gone dry. Cripes! You turned on the faucet and anything would come through!

The first Community Day in Staatsburg was put on in 1949 by Len Zneimer and the school association—the P. T. A. The Zneimers lived at the Anderson School when Len was a teacher there and his kids, Annette and Eddie, went to Staatsburg School until about fourth or fifth grade. Then Lenny opened up the school in Rhinebeck and they moved up there.

Community Day was not a drinking party in those days. They had things to do all over the village. We had an art exhibit at the school and Faye Emerson and Mrs. Roosevelt were there. This was a well-done affair. Len was president of the P. T. A. and he did a good job when he did it. They had the pet show, and the school band played. You could eat out at Norrie Point, too. Norrie was really a place to eat in those days. Wonderful food down there. You really got a good meal.

It was an active little community, I thought.

Part Two

In this section Mr. Stewart discusses making the Staatsburg School part of the Hyde Park School District in 1961.

We stayed out of the central school district for twenty years—wanted no part of it. The state started to put more things in—we had to have shop, we had to have homemaking. We had this north corner of the school that had been a coal bin. After we put in oil burners, we made the coal bin the industrial arts shop. And we took about two-thirds of the library and made that the homemaking room; cut our library down. That pacified the state. They were after us every year to centralize or do this or do that, but we ignored them. That's what you have to do with the state is ignore them. We kept them happy and they stayed away from us.

As a matter of fact, one of the reasons we stayed out of the central district for twenty years was Franklin Roosevelt. You see, Harry Barker was a big Republican and one night he went to a meeting where they were talking about centralization. The state had said the central high school should be here in Staatsburg in as much as we already had the building here. Roosevelt stood up and said, "The high school is going to be in Hyde Park, not in Staatsburg, in Hyde Park!" Harry Barker said, "The Staatsburg School will never be in Hyde Park. It will be in Staatsburg." And for twenty years we stayed right here.

Finally, though, it was so crowded it did get to the point where we had classes on the stage, and up in the balcony. As a matter of fact, we used the girls' restrooms and the boys' restrooms for some small classes. We may have been teaching more than we had to at the time—French, Spanish, Latin—more than Rhinebeck or Hyde Park. They were only teaching two languages when we were teaching three. We were teaching all the science and math courses. The kids needed and wanted these courses and I put them in for them. Even though some of the classes weren't too big, I had the teachers who could teach them, so we did it. I had some teachers teaching six periods a day. That's not too much—you might just as well be teaching a class as sitting in the teachers' room having a smoke or cutting someone else's throat.

Well, we just had too many kids so we went to the State Education Department with a set of plans to add on to the north end of the elementary school. An architect, Ralph Dryer who started the Clark and Warren Architectural firm, went up with us. We went over these plans with the state and they said we really needed thirteen rooms, but we couldn't have them because of the cost. I told them, "The people of Staatsburg want this addition to the building. They want to stay in Staatsburg." He told me, "No, you can't have it." They thought it was too much money.

At that time, Hyde Park didn't want us so some board members went to Poughkeepsie to see if they would take our eleventh and twelfth graders. They said they would, but we had done that years before and it really wasn't satisfactory.

We had a meeting with the Rhinebeck board to see if they could help us. Gilmour was up there then and he told us they'd "make a study of the situation." We sent him the information and about a month later we got word that they were not interested in helping us.

Shortly after that, Hyde Park said they might be able to do something for us so we met a couple of times and we decided we all wanted to do something about centralization. Walt Clifford and I went up to Albany and they showed us some new regulations. If Hyde Park went together with Staatsburg, Hyde Park could start all over again on their state aid for building. See, they had used up their quota; they would not have gotten any more. But, if they went in with us, they'd get a million dollars more. Staatsburg, though, would not have to assume any of Hyde Park's debt. Our building was all paid off—we had just burned up our mortgage. Well, this was an ideal situation for Hyde Park and it would cost the people of Staatsburg nothing, so our board was for it.

Now the problem was to sell it to the people. That was a tough job because they didn't want any part of it. They wanted the school right here. The two school boards wondered what to do about publicity. Ed Rosell at the Poughkeepsie paper was a friend of mine and when the boards came up with the story of the centralization, I brought it down to him, and Ed put it in the paper exactly as the school boards had worded it. The State Education Department couldn't believe that it went through so well with the public.

The two school boards worked it out well and gave the people a lot of information. I think there were a lot of unhappy people but it did go through. I think to the present time some are still unhappy—they wanted a school here, you know.

I think it turned out for the best for the kids. They had a bigger school to go to. Of course, for the first two years down at Roosevelt at graduation, the valedictorian and the salutatorian came from the Staatsburg School. As I said, I had a good faculty and they worked hard.

Every year our kids came out on top in the state science and math tests. We were number one in the district. One time after I had retired I went in to school to say hello to the teachers. One of them said, "Mr. Stewart, I'd like you to meet our new assistant superintendent."

He said, "Oh, you're the fellow who had such good results on all these state tests. I was just wondering—who corrected those papers?" (This is the brains—the assistant superintendent!)

"Well," I said, "the teachers did most of them. I helped out, and if you had been here you could have corrected some. It wouldn't have made any difference.!"

He said, "Oh," and just walked on.

Later in his office he said, "How come you had such good results with these kids?"

I said, "Do you really want to know?"

"Yeah, I'd like to know."

I said, "To begin with, we all used the same textbook. In the second place, my teachers teach and were in the classroom when they were supposed to be. They were not in the halls; they were not in the teachers' room; they were not cutting each other's throats; they were working; they were teaching when they were supposed to be. If teachers will do that, they won't have any trouble teaching and kids will learn."

He said, "Oh." He never said anything more and I never heard from him or spoke to him again. But, every year our kids were on top, and it was the faculty. They did a good job of teaching.

'Course at the time I became principal, there were no married female teachers here at the Staatsburg School. As soon as they got married that was it—they had to leave. I went to board meeting after board meeting about hiring married teachers. I said I can see where the married teachers would be better than the single ones. The married gals would be home at night taking care of the house and family; they've got things to do. But these young gals come around here, there, out and around town and you never know where they are or when they're home, or what they're doing. I told the board I leaned toward hiring the married gals. It was quite some time before I got them to consent to let me hire married ones. They said, "O. K., you can hire married women, but you be responsible."

The first one I tried to hire was Eva Kuhn. She was an excellent teacher who had had to quit because she had gotten married. I went after Eva but they had just given her a job in Rhinebeck as a supervisor of elementary teachers. I got her a couple of years later anyway. Eva is a good teacher.

Fortunately, I had a good board who said, "You're running the school—you run it. And when you can't run it, we'll get somebody who can." So I usually told the parents what I wanted to tell them. I think what helped was I knew these kids. I had coached some baseball teams and some basketball teams, and I think they trusted me. They believed what I said. That's all—if they believe you. If they don't believe you.....

Parents knew what to expect from me over the years. Some of my students grew up to be parents in town. They knew it was no sense in talking to Stewart because he'll defend his teachers. I said, "That's right." I used to tell them, "If you can prove to me that a teacher did something wrong, I'll do something about it. But until you do, the teacher's right. The kid's wrong." The parents understood that.

I used paddles. I had all kinds of paddles. I had one kid who came in one day in trouble. Bucky Taber was the janitor in those days. I told this kid, "You go down and tell Mr. Taber I want him to make a paddle I can use on you." God, he went down and he was gone about forty-five minutes. When he came back, he was white as a sheet. I never did use a paddle on him; he'd a died if I had. I used to swat them a few times. They got a kick out of it.

One night I had these four kids come in. I was in my office with the football coach who was about 230 pounds. I said, "These kids need to be paddled."

The coach said, "I'd like to do that."

I said, "Go ahead, I'll watch." Well, the kids wanted to put boards and pans and stuff down their trousers. He took each kid and gave them three or four swats. He made a big thing of it, and the kids got a big kick out of it.

After we had centralized, Walt Clifford, the superintendent, told me he didn't think any teacher should have to hit a kid. I told Clifford, "Wait, when a kid is in front of me and giving me a little lip, the most effective way to handle him is to give him a little cuff right across the kisser. I've done this many times. Or grab him and give him a good shaking and straighten him out." And I said, "I'm for it and I'll never criticize any teachers unless they get abusive—that's one thing. But just to grab a-hold of a kid, I'll never say anything."

One of the things that has hurt education is that they have taken away from the school people the authority to deal with the kids. When I was in school, they told you what to do. Now the kids turn around and say, "You can't tell me what to do!" The last year I was at the school it was just starting. A kid came in and said, "The teacher can't hit me."

"No," I said, "But I want to tell you something. While you're here, the teacher is the boss, not you. And if she doesn't hit you,

I'm liable to. So remember that! And go home and tell that to your mother."

You can't suspend a kid from school until you bring in his attorney. This is nonsense! If a kid does something wrong, you should kick him out and tell him not to come back until his parents straighten him out. Then we wouldn't have this drug and drinking problem with kids.

My feeling is that kids getting out of school today know more than kids ever knew getting out of school. I don't think it's because of the teaching necessarily; I think it's because of everything—T.V., the news media, the newspaper. You get so much more news today. Kids travel so much more. Our transportation is so much better. These are the things that help education.

Perhaps some of the teaching is not as good as it was because I don't think the teachers are that interested, but I think the kids are learning. They are teaching a lot more than we ever knew. I hear my grandchildren talk about the work they do, and in math it's work you never heard of! And biology they used to teach to seniors, they're teaching to seventh graders now. People don't realize this. Look at the history they've had to cover in the last forty years. There is no comparison between what the kids have to learn in school today and what we learned in school.

I had a good time at the Staatsburg School reunion a few years ago. I saw kids I hadn't seen in years. One of the worst kids in school had become a minister. And a couple of others are teachers. One is a vice-president of IBM. That's Walt Benson—used to live right up the street here. He got an athletic scholarship to NYU when he graduated. Walt was a good kid.

I think I got out of education at the right time. About forty years ago I said there were three things that were going to ruin our

country: news media, unions, and the "do-gooders." Everything that comes up the "do-gooders" are going to change. And the news media have been trying to get Reagan for years and now they're after Nancy. Show me another country where the news media can cause a president to resign. They got Nixon out.

And I got out of education before teacher negotiations. Phil Cookingham and the board of education decided the salaries in my time. We got about $25 or $50 a year raise. Then one year when I was principal, they asked me to come up with a salary schedule for my teachers. I only had 18 or 20 teachers so I knew who was working and who wasn't. I made up a schedule based on individuals and what kind of raise I thought they should get. It was a big increase over what they were usually given. I brought it to the board and they adopted it. A few years later the state came out with a salary schedule to pay teachers. I think as a principal I started at $2600 a year and as a teacher I started at $1300.

I've had a good time. I've enjoyed it. That's why I stayed as long as I did. I was here thirty-seven years. Thirty as principal. I retired in 1971. It got a little monotonous with not enough to do. When you have a good faculty, you don't have to do anything.

I like Staatsburg, and my wife liked it here, too. I had chances to go other places, but I stayed here until I retired because I like Staatsburg.

August 1983

Birgit Crusius

Mrs. Crusius is a dignified and gracious woman who has lived in Staatsburg for almost seventy years. I interviewed her in the house she shares with her daughter on Mountain View Road.

At eighty-three years old, Mrs. Crusius is justifiably proud of the contributions she has made to Staatsburg by being our librarian for many years and an active participant in the congregation of St. Margaret's Episcopal Church.

Photographs, newspaper clippings, and other memorabilia were shared with me, as Birgit Crusius helped me to understand the village as it was many years ago.

"Hold faithfulness and sincerity as first principles."
—CONFUCIUS

MY FAMILY IS FROM NORWAY. We came to America to live in Mobile, Alabama. My father worked on dredging out the Mississippi River. Eventually, we moved to West Park, New York, across the river from here, because the climate in the South was not healthy for my mother. We came to West Park so that my father could work on Colonel Payne's estate.

Miss Carson was the housekeeper at Colonel Payne's house, and when he died she received a great deal of money. She bought the big white house across Route 9 from the village of Staatsburg, near Mills Cross Road. She asked my father to work for her. So we came to Staatsburg in 1919.

When I was younger, the village was a lovely place. There were manicured sidewalks throughout the town. There was an ice cream parlor on the side porch of Horan's Hotel. There was also an ice cream shop at Millard's next to the old post office. They made homemade ice cream. We had a butcher store across from Borner's and another grocery store in that house across from the new post office.

The town hall was on Mulford Avenue. We could go there to watch silent movies. We also put on school plays there. I remember one year I was a rainbow. My mother colored strips of gauze to wrap around me. I received many compliments about that costume. Anyway, the sidewalks and streets were very well cared for in those days. They had horse-drawn plows to clear the snow.

I remember what it was like when the river froze over. We did a lot of ice boating. When we lived in West Park, we could walk across the river to Hyde Park. I will never forget what happened to me when I was about ten years old. It was winter and my mother sent me to Poughkeepsie to buy some things. Usually I would take a train from West Park to Highland, and from there a ferry would take me to Poughkeepsie. However, this time when I arrived in Highland I found that the ferry was not running, so I walked all the way across the river on the ice to Poughkeepsie. In my hand I was clutching a little satchel with ten dollars in it. I remember how my hand was frozen around that satchel by the time I reached the city. Then I found out they were having a "heatless Monday." This meant that all the stores were closed! We did not know about such things because we rarely got newspapers. I had to turn around and walk all the way back across the river to Highland. By this time it was snowing very hard, and it was getting late. I really was scared. I kept thinking of the story that was going around about a wildcat being loose in the area. My mother was so worried about me that she sent my brother out with a pair of skis to find me. He had heard the stories about the wildcat, too, so he went to a neighbor's house instead of coming after me! I finally made it home in snow that was up to my knees.

In the nice weather in Staatsburg we had a baseball game in town every single Sunday. It was often Hyde Park against Staatsburg. And every single time they played, the same two men had a huge argument. Also, there were four girls who used to walk around on Sundays dressed to kill!

The train station was always a very busy place. The Mills family used to rent their own private train car to come to their estate. They would pull the cars over to a rail spur when they arrived, and then hook them back up to a train when they were ready to return to the city. Miss Phipps always arrived in town with a poodle tucked under her arm.

Dr. Herridon would make house calls for $2 in those days. They say that my husband's mother was the first patient he ever lost. She died of pneumonia when my husband was very young. But the doctor saved William's father from a very serious case of blood poisoning. No matter what was wrong with you, though, Dr. Herridon managed to make five house calls for your illness! He had spells of some kind. In fact he was killed when his car went off the road during one of his spells.

The original school in Staatsburg only went to tenth grade. If you wanted to finish high, you had to take a train from the village to Poughkeepsie. From the train station in the city, you had to walk up to the school that is now Our Lady of Lourdes. I did not go four years to high school. I went to two years of high school and then the Eastman Gaines Business School. From there I worked for five years in New York City at the public library. A friend of Miss Larson's arranged the job for me. I really did not like New York. The food was terrible on my delicate stomach. It was quite an adventure, but I returned home to Staatsburg.

My husband, Bill, did finish high school and then went on to the Eastman Business School. He went to work at Mr. Doughty's gas station and car dealership. It was located in that lot next to the firehouse in the center of the village. That was around 1930.

The people on the estates were always very generous to the churches in Staatsburg. I was married at St. Margaret's on Easter Sunday. I did not even have to buy flowers for the altar because every Easter and Christmas, the estate owners would send large beautiful plants and flowers to decorate the church. I have been a member of

St. Margaret's for over sixty years and worked on many committees for the church.

Bill and I built this house in 1927. It was surrounded by orchards and hay fields. It is on four acres, and none of the houses on this street were here at that time, of course.

Staatsburg has changed a lot.

February 1987

Leonard Peluso

Len Peluso is an energetic, intense man with a shock of white hair who has been active in community organizations and activities since he came to Staatsburg almost forty years ago. Although he is retired from his profession as a nurse at Hudson River State Psychiatric Center, Len was a difficult man to schedule for an interview because he continues to be so busy with his many volunteer commitments.

During the course of our interview, I learned a great deal about what the city of Poughkeepsie was like many years ago, and about the evolution of mental health care. Mostly though, we talked about the changes in Staatsburg—the village where Len and his wife, Rena, came in 1948 to live in the house where Rena was born.

"The reward of a thing well done is to have done it."
—EMERSON

I FIRST CAME TO STAATSBURG when we were only kids and we played baseball here and went to Norrie Park. We used to have picnics from St. Peter's School in Poughkeepsie. We would come up, spend the day, go swimming, and then go home. All the elementary schools had their little teams and rivalries—and we enjoyed that.

My wife was born in the house we live in now, on River Road. Her father worked on the railroad, but in his spare time he worked as a cobbler. Like most of the people who came over to this country, idleness wasn't in his vocabulary. On the corner of Railroad Avenue and River Road, next to that house, was a little building that is not there now. That was his shoe shop. We still have the equipment he used. It's over one hundred years old.

Mrs. Hull always came down to his shop. Even when he stopped the business, she used to come down to the house asking for Mr. Porfirio to do her shoes. He learned his trade in the old country, just like my father learned his trade over there.

My father came over in 1885. He had had a thriving business over there. First he came to Brooklyn and around 1895 he brought his family to Poughkeepsie where my uncle lived. I think there were only three or four Italian families in Poughkeepsie at that time.

We came across some of my father's papers not too long ago. He paid about $85 for three barber chairs, assortment of other chairs, and all the barber equipment. All for $85! That was down at Cataract Square and then they changed the name to Mt. Carmel. I came from a family of nine boys and four girls and our family has been in the house in Poughkeepsie since 1910. Before that we were in a house one block away.

My father supported us all as a barber, and did a good job because most of us got a college education. It was during the Depression that it was really hard because we were all at the age where we wanted to go on to more education. He said, "If you want it, you'll have to work for it yourself." He taught us this trade—that was a must for him. His philosophy was this (and it still holds true today, regardless of what anybody tells you): "You learn this trade. You can follow it if you want, and then go do what you want."

But, we had to learn his trade. That was a must and I don't think we were any taller than knee-high to a grasshopper when we started helping out in the barbershop. We had a little bench—I'm going way back before your time when they had a little stool to get on board a train—that's what we used to stand on to reach the customer—that's how small we were. We'd lather them up and save my father time. We had three chairs in the shop, my father and my brothers all working. Of course he was the kingpin. We'd lather them up, he'd finish one customer and come over, and we'd move on to the next one.

We were probably the original assembly line! I had one job to do and he had a job to do and so did each of my brothers. Anyway, we all learned the trade. 'Course we used to get a penny on Sunday, but we had chores to do. We had to clean the barbershop, oil floors, do whatever we had to do to make sure everything was clean. On top of that we had a shoeshine set up in the front to kind of supplement the pennies he gave us. Don't forget, he had a lot of kids. Haircuts and shaves were not as expensive then as they are today—15 cents and 25 cents. That's where you heard the phrase, "shave and a haircut—two bits."

We all worked in the shop at one time or another and my two oldest brothers went on to become barbers. Another brother, who went to the University of Pennsylvania, got a scholarship for boxing, but he also earned his way in college by working Saturdays and Sundays in a barbershop. John and I did the same thing when we went into nursing. We got paid, I think, $21 a month in training, but then I spent a year training at Bellvue Hospital and there I got nothing. So, I used to cut hair for a quarter. That was after we got through working, and after we did our studying—we cut hair. 'Cause as I said, we didn't get any help from home. My father just couldn't afford it. Most of the education we got, we had to fight for. So we all learned the trade except my youngest brother. My father was getting a little old then and he just didn't have the patience to each him.

When we were busy, it was all business. But, I remember the barbershop was like a gathering place on a Saturday night. Somebody was always musically inclined. My uncle used to play the mandolin.

It was a little different than it is today. Then, everybody was one big conglomerate of friends in the neighborhood. One whole block was mostly Italian; then another block farther up was Poles; and there were some Irish, too. Before we got there the whole area was German. And, in those days you had your own schools, too. I went to St. Peter's and one block away, what is now HVOIC, was #9, the Franklin School. Both schools were within a block of each other, and everybody knew everybody. Those teachers knew my father because it was an old tradition in Italy not to charge the priests for a haircut, so they were always coming into the shop for a haircut and if we had misbehaved in school, my father would know about it right away.

It was a different way of life then. We used to enjoy walking in Poughkeepsie up to what is now Marist College's dormitories to the north where Dutchess Bank is on Route 9. Then it was an amusement park--Woodcliffe. You would never know it but there was a lake there and an amusement park. That was at least fifty years ago. We used to get in for 10 cents and of course we'd spend the whole day there. It had an amusement park atmosphere with all the various games and rides—a Ferris wheel and a roller coaster and a caterpillar.

They had a ballroom for dance marathons; they were in vogue then. And they had roller skating marathons, too. We watched some very famous wrestlers who came to Woodcliffe—Jim Londos and I think they had Primo Cannaro. The ballroom burned down. There was a restaurant at the park, too.

They built Woodcliffe at the wrong time—the Depression—but people used to come from New York on an excursion boat. It was a regular amusement park. Then there was a riot of some kind one day during the Depression and that put the kibosh on the place.

I worked at Hudson River State Hospital for forty-two years. I met my wife there when she was the head nurse on Employee Sick Bay. I had gone off to the service, and when I came back in 1946, I saw this woman in charge of upstairs. I was in charge of the surgical ward downstairs and that's how we got together. In fact, the first date we went out on was Valentine's Day. That was over thirty-nine years ago. We were married in 1948 and soon after moved into the village of Staatsburg.

There are a lot of things about Staatsburg that are hard to believe.

When I first came here they had stores, hotels, trains, buses, sidewalks. That's something I really miss now—sidewalks along Old Post Road. We always watched out for the kids when we were driving to work, and the principal of the school made sure they stayed on the sidewalks, too. Today there are no sidewalks anywhere in town. I think they just went to pot and disintegrated. Roland Kilmer had a "V" plow with a horse pulling it, and he would clear the sidewalk from what is now Chiaramonte's all the way up into town.

There was a Cadillac and Packard automobile dealer on the corner next to the firehouse. The barber was right next to the tracks on River Road. Across the tracks was the creamery that Bodenstein owned. There was a soda fountain and Millard's soda shop, a butcher shop, a tavern, the post office, and other stores all right in the village. I also remember Bingo parties, card parties, and Saturday night dances at the firehouse.

We used to have ball games every Sunday. They had bleachers up for the people to watch the games. There was a fella here who lived, drank, and worked baseball—Walt Benson. He used to keep our field immaculate and up to date. You couldn't even find a pebble on the place. He spent all his time at the field and he was an avid baseball fan. It was all voluntary. Of course, all these things we get paid for today were voluntary in those days. There was more camaraderie because everyone knew everybody.

The centers of activity were your churches and the firehouse. We had three churches in Staatsburg—St. Paul's Catholic Church, St. Margaret's Episcopal Church, and the Bethel Methodist Church. It was quite an active community. On Community Day we'd start out with a kiddie pet parade and lots of little games but by 5 o'clock it was all over.

When I came to the village, I joined the fire company, and I became a fire commissioner in 1960. I was on there for fifteen years. While I was chairman of the board of fire commissioners, my wife had an accident and fell off the porch at home. I was working at the state hospital and I got a call to get up to Staatsburg quick! At that time the village didn't have an ambulance or rescue squad. I beat the ambulance from a local hospital up to our house and my wife was just laying there. In those days the hospitals did not have the ambulances and trained people they have today. They were just workers who would drive the ambulance.

Well, when they got to my house they were going to pick my wife up. I told them they weren't going to pick her up with a back injury! This was the kind of training they didn't have. I mean you really can't blame them. This was the modus operandi then. I said, "You're not going to touch her. You bring that blankety-blank stretcher over here!" They weren't trained to handle the sick. The old term for ambulance was "meat wagon." If I hadn't been there, I'm sure my wife would be paralyzed today.

Then I said to myself, well, it's about time we got something here in Staatsburg. So we had the lovely women from the Methodist Church run food sales and of course Bill Utter's contribution is very well known. I met with a lot of opposition, believe me. I was called everything, but I felt the people were entitled to more than just a fire truck.

Art Flanagan, Jim Horan, and myself started out our rescue squad with a station wagon, a tank of oxygen, and a first-aid kit. That was how we started in 1968. That's how we responded to the calls.

We went through the whole area for money for an ambulance. The Utters, the women from the Methodist Church, Mrs. Ackert, and quite a few more people all helped out. I remember bake sales out in front of the firehouse. Some people said a rescue squad was going to cost too much, but not a single penny we got came out of the town or any place else. Two years after we started the rescue squad, we were able to buy a second-hand ambulance.

They were offering EMS courses at Dutchess Community College so Art and I went and took a course and we came back here and started from scratch. I gave first-aid training and eventually we had as many as twenty or twenty-five volunteers on the squad.

We had an awful lot of support from the people in Staatsburg for a rescue squad because they thought it was worthwhile. In the beginning we only had about eight or ten calls for the year and now we average in the hundreds.

Staatsburg was quite an active community and at one time most of these people worked on the estates. Then, with the closing of the estates, everyone moved out. They all came down to Poughkeepsie for work. And when everybody started to have a car, the village wasn't the center of activities anymore. Also, stores and businesses started closing down when they put in the bypass around the village. Like Poughkeepsie when they put the arterial in, they bypassed all the little Mom and Pop shops that made their business on people going to work and stopping for coffee or a paper. When they bypassed them, there goes the business. Like everything else, when you put something like that in, something else dies.

February 1987

Marion Asher

During the course of a recent discussion with a long-time Staatsburg resident, he remarked with some pride, "Oh, Marion Asher is our Vassar girl, you know."

Although one would not necessarily have learned that fact from Marion, it is obvious from looking through Staatsburg School memorabilia of the 1930s that she had been a class leader and a scholar. A reserved and thoughtful woman, Marion retains those qualities of her youth during her retirement from the Hyde Park School System. She has served for many years on the Staatsburg Library Board of Directors in the village and always works to improve the local visual environment. Recently, she was involved in planting thousands of flowers and bushes at the restored Vanderbilt gardens.

An avid amateur historian, Marion recognizes the importance of preserving the buildings, trees, traditions, and memories of people in the Staatsburg area. Her narrative provides the unique perspective of a resident who left Staatsburg after college and returned almost twenty years later with her husband and children to the large white farmhouse where she had lived with parents across from the Staatsburg School on Old Post Road.

During her absence, the village had changed a great deal, and recently Marion was able to reflect on those changes with both sentiment and candor.

> "Nothing endures but change."
> –HERACHTUS

MY PARENTS MOVED TO STAATSBURG from Albany in 1938. My father was a horticultural inspector for New York State and was given the territory of Westchester and Dutchess, so they decided they wanted to be here to live.

Both the stone house and the home my parents bought were vacant when my parents were driving up and down looking at houses in this area. They would look across the fields and see this house. I think more than the village of Staatsburg, they really loved the house and all the land. There is ten acres, and my father loved a lot of land so he could garden—plant apple trees. They liked to be out in the country. Finally they found someone who knew something about the house and they got to rent it.

After a year, my parents, the Goolds, made an offer to buy the house from Miss Madeline Dinsmore. I think she lived in Boston at the time, and I still have letters about the sale of the property which are addressed to Martin W. Hayes, who managed the Dinsmore Estate.

The Dinsmores owned everything around here at one time. They owned the golf course, the water company, and all the land along Old Post Road up to where the school property is now. They owned the stone house and of course the Dinsmore Estate which was called "The Locusts." The house on that estate was torn down by Helen Huntington Astor when she divorced Vincent Astor and married her journalist husband, Lytle Hull. They built a new house, and the current estate is owned by Bob Guccione now.

There was a relationship of some kind between the Huntingtons and the Dinsmores. That's how Helen Huntington Astor got the

Dinsmore property—she was related to the Dinsmores in some way. The Dinsmore property and the Huntington property joined each other.

I did some research on the house my parents bought and I found out that before the Dinsmores owned it, it was a part of a working farm owned by George Lamoree. Mr. Lamoree lived in the stone house and he built our house for his son to live in. Farming was a family business for the Lamorees. In my safe I have the deed from the original sale of the house.

When my parents moved here the stone house was vacant, also. My cousin Rachel Shreve came to visit us from New York City and she fell in love with it. She ended up buying the house from Miss Dinsmore. So they were the first people to own it after the Dinsmores. They were the ones who first restored it. They painted it white, which I am always regretful of, because it was a lovely shade of peachy-pink before it was painted.

Many years before my parents even considered living in Staatsburg, my husband's relatives, the Kipps, rented the stone house from the Dinsmores. In fact, my husband was born there. His mother lived on Long Island, but she came up to her mother's house to have her child. Isn't that amazing that we ended up here? It's crazy.

When I think of first moving into the village in 1938, it was a thriving community. There was a sense of community about it. The churches were active—the Methodist Church across form the old post office, the Catholic Church on Mulford Avenue, and the Episcopal Church on East Elm Avenue.

The Methodist Church is a private home now, but it was the church I went to. We had Sunday School, church suppers, and I was in the choir. I remember Miss Gladys Hennion—the Hennions lived in the big house that used to be in the open field as you come into Staatsburg. It was where the state has a fitness trail now. Miss Hennion was a member of the church choir and always graced us with "The Palms" on Palm Sunday in her high soprano voice. I will remember that for as long as I live. Everybody had to sit calmly and wait for it to end!

The town was thriving. There were two grocery stores at one time, believe it or not. There was the one run by Wilfred Borner that we always called the Miles Hughes Estate Store. It came from the Hughes Estate, but I don't know the history of that. The other store was Ackerman's which was in the last building on Market Street, across from the present post office. This was in the 1940s and both stores were apparently prospering. On the same side of Market Street, in that row of stores, was Johnny Millard's Ice Cream Parlor. Millard's had the little round tables with the ice cream parlor chairs and the fountain with the marble top. He would make you an ice cream soda.

There was a shoe repair shop and a wonderful barbershop and Schouten's Meat Market. I'm sure we bought all our meat at Schouten's. You got good quality meat form a good butcher. You didn't need to go anyplace else to shop. They lived in that big gray house up along Old Post Road. It was taken down by the state. By the 1940s, the only boarding houses that were left in Staatsburg were up on Route 9— Stone's Farm and Whitewall Manor. Mostly people from New York City would come up there to stay and had no association with the village; maybe come for a walk through the village, but that was it.

Where the empty lot is now, next to the firehouse, was a garage. Then it became a milk truck sub-station for the C & E Trucking Company, which was a very disagreeable thing because the great big tank trucks would come lumbering up and down the road. That was the last thing that happened in that building and then I guess they took it down.

There has always been a great deal of rivalry between Hyde Park and Staatsburg. It's just something that is there. When I first moved here as a kid, you felt this sense of rivalry. Of course, at one time Staatsburg was certainly the equal of Hyde Park. That was in the very old days, maybe at the turn of the century, when Staatsburg had a town hall and many businesses. I think they were equal communities.

When I came here in 1938, the Staatsburg Union School served Hyde Park kids. All the kids form Hyde Park came up here for their four years of high school. I believe 1940 was the last year they came up here.

It was great having a small class. We had good teachers, and the principal at that time was Gaylord Hakes who was a very well thought of man. When he left, Ken Stewart became principal. I remember my teachers very well. They all knew you, took a personal interest in you, and did special things with you.

I remember when I was a kid in high school, I would go with my friends into Poughkeepsie on the bus that came right through the village—the Twilight Bus Company from Red Hook. It was good bus service and you could go into Poughkeepsie for a movie or shopping. The railroad station was in Staatsburg, too, and there was excellent train service at that time. People used to commute all the time. It was wonderful—just wonderful!!

To get to Norrie Park (not the state park, the one the village owned), you would walk on that road down to the river and first of all you would come upon the monument with the inscription about Lewis Gordon Norrie. Then you would wind down the hill and come to the house where Mr. Hinds lived with his family. He was the caretaker of the park.

I remember it being a good place to swim. The water was clear, and you didn't think twice about swimming in the river in those days. It's completely changed. I don't know, almost the land seems to have altered. It doesn't look at all like it used to.

I went away to school in 1943 and was only here for the summers. I was married in 1948 and left entirely so it's hard for me to remember exactly what happened when, and how things changed during that time. I came back into the village to live in 1966, when my father died. My husband and I and our family came to live in the house and we built the apartment over the garage for my mother. The village had changed so much by then that it was almost like I felt like disassociating myself from it. I didn't even feel like I was a part of the village anymore. In fact, I have a whole different feeling about it now when I go to the post office and see all the different people I don't know. You don't see the same faces; you see them one year and the next year they're gone. It's just not the same feeling at all that it had then, when you knew everybody. Things do change.

I think the state taking over the land along the river was very hard for the village in the short run, but in the long run the fact that we have access to the river in so many places and the land is protected—I'm all for that. I think we need to preserve green area, especially around the Hudson River. I was not here at the time, but I think people really began to be upset about the state taking Mrs. Hoyt's house when they saw what an awful thing was being done to this historically significant house by just letting it set there and decay away. Originally the state talked about putting a swimming pool in up there as part of the park.

I don't really know why so many people left Staatsburg. I think the school situation changed things, and the change must be based on the economics. I suppose when I came in 1938, it was the tailend of the thriving estates. The railroad station was there because the Huntingtons and Dinsmores and Mills all had to come up here from New York City. But the train stopped coming; the roads got worse so the bus company finally said they wouldn't come through anymore. Mrs. Astor was the only one left on the big estates. The village was a service community to the estates, and when they closed, nothing

came along to replace them economically. People simply didn't move into Staatsburg anymore. And when you no longer have the people, the stores close.

So, I guess my family came at the beginning of the decline of the village. After the estates closed, the war came and after the war I think everybody wanted a new house. There was not the same emphasis on saving old buildings as there is now. People did not treasure old houses. If you had an old house with a porch, you took the porch off to modernize your house! There was a whole new feeling after the war, and I just think people didn't think about these old communities in the same way. There was no reason to stay here so a period of gradual decay set in, almost to the point where it was too late to pull it back. Once the process of decay begins, it seems like it is almost irreversible.

It breaks your heart to think about walking up the road, and to remember the tree-lined village streets and how lovely they were.

1987

Oliver Goring

Oliver Goring met with me at his son, Jim's, house on Hughes Avenue in Staatsburg. Mr. Goring has lived in Hyde Park for most of his life, and he and his wife, Ann, actively support and work for the historic preservation of the town.

Because he attended high school in Staatsburg and worked in this area delivering ice, Mr. Goring was able to provide a viewpoint of Staatsburg from the perspective of someone who was connected with the village, but not really a resident for any length of time.

Although we had never met before our taped discussion, I found Oliver Goring to be extremely cooperative and enthusiastic and I found him to be quite introspective about national and local events that had influenced his youth. I particularly appreciated Mr. Goring's sense of humor about Hyde Park, Staatsburg, and even himself.

Work consists of whatever a body is obliged to do.
Play consists of whatever a body is not obliged to do."
–Mark Twain

I LIVED IN HYDE PARK for most of my life and went to Staatsburg School in 1934, 35, 36. I had gone to Hyde Park Elementary but it only went up to two years of high school. That was a brick two-story building located where the Getty Station is now on Route 9. It had eight grades plus two years of high school. Until 1934, Hyde Park kids went to Poughkeepsie High to finish their education. Then Staatsburg built the new school that went all the way through four years of high school, so Hyde Park kids went there for their last two years.

When I went to school in Staatsburg, Ken Stewart was the coach. Irwin L. Baker was the principal at that time. Evelyn Bradt taught French, Margaret Carbury taught English, and Walwoth taught commercial arithmetic.

Tom Steenson was one of the better athletes—a very good basketball player. Harry Hess and Roswell Taber played baseball and basketball. In those small schools you played both baseball and basketball. The school wasn't big enough for football. Bob Baker, Nelson Kidder, Bill Kiernan, Bob and Tommy Gilbert all played on teams here. They had a good girls' basketball team, too. Anna Sinibaldi, Bea Davidson, Lena Profirio, Vicky Osika, Mildred Gallon all were good basketball players from Staatsburg.

There was always a bit of rivalry between Hyde Park and Staatsburg, but when we came up to school here we got along fine. We all worked together. We had a lot of plays and shows that we put on. I can remember one of the dances in the Spring. At intermission a whole bunch of us went down to the river swimming. We came back with our hair all wet. The teachers didn't know we had our bathing suits. To this day some of them think we went swimming "a la Mother Nature." We went down to the old Norrie Park. We were used to roaming around in the dark. It's not like it is today—everything lighted, and we were used to the river. We grew up on the river.

I had grown up canoeing on the Hudson. We used to camp in that cove around the corner from Bard Rock in Hyde Park. In fact they're building a house there now and it makes me mad! In the canoe we'd go across the river to Colonel Payne's—over to the red-roofed boathouse—and swim there on the beach, and we would go up to the Dominican Camp.

In those days the Dominican Camp had both boys and girls. The girls were on the river side and we used to go paddling up the river. I had a portable Victrola and we'd serenade the girls and try to get them to come out. It didn't work. We'd talk to them, that's all, and then someone would come and chase us.

I don't know where the rivalry between the two villages started. It started before my time. Some of the guys who were older than me used to play football every Thanksgiving. There was Fritz Gilbert, the Seavers, Herb Saltford. In Staatsburg there was Bud Hess, and I think one of the Bodensteins, and some other guys. They played football and baseball and there was rivalry between them. Don't ask me why. I think it was just a sport rivalry. I don't think it evolved from boys from Hyde Park stealing Staatsburg girls, or Staatsburg boys stealing Hyde Park girls, or anything like that.

I can't tell you where the nickname "zoo" came from, either. It was just a funny nickname—"zooburgers" we used to call them. And then I became a "zooburger" myself! Staatsburg just didn't seem to be as active as Hyde Park was, youthwise. We used to jokingly say it was the only cemetery in the United States with lights in it. We just seemed to have more going on down in Hyde Park but maybe they had as much going up in here in Staatsburg. I don't know. I never got too involved except through school activities like sports and plays and things. I didn't really hang out here.

I think Roosevelt High School was built in 1941 and that ended the Hyde Park kids coming up here to high school. Then years later the Hyde Park system took in the Staatsburg kids. That was in the 1960s.

Around 1933, 34, 35 or 36, I'm a little hazy about the dates, I peddled ice through Staatsburg. In the village and out through Pleasant Plains, down Quaker Lane and down River Road. You went down to Poughkeepsie and bought ice—300 pound cakes of ice—and you'd load them in a truck. We bought it from Wilber, who's out of business now. You had a regular route, and you went around and put ice in people's iceboxes.

I was on the tag end of the ice business. It wasn't during the glory days when they harvested ice on the river or on ponds, although I did that the first year. I worked for Leonard Travis and he had a pond and an icehouse. He had natural ice there and I did haul it out of the icehouse. It was located where Vanderbilt Acres is now in Hyde Park. There was a pond back in there and old Len Travis used to get ice from it and fill his icehouse which was right where the road goes into Vanderbilt Acres. It's all torn down now. But, after that first year it was much easier to just go to Poughkeepsie and get the ice where they manufactured it.

One of my favorite places to deliver ice in Staatsburg was Johnny Millard's. He had a little ice cream store down in the village. It was a little bit of a place. He made his own syrups and he had the best syrups of any place I ever went. But he was a crusty old son of a gun. Oh, yeah, he was crotchety. He was an Englishman and still had a little accent.

When you delivered to houses, you came right into the kitchen, or the people would have a box out on the back porch or entryway where you left the ice. There was one place I remember on the road that's closed off now—the River Road. It was Mrs. Clark's, and she was one of my favorites because she always had a glass of iced tea in the icebox for me or for whoever delivered the ice.

And there was another family named Melius that lived out on Quaker Lane that I always got a piece of pie from. They had a boarding house. There were a lot of places out there that took summer boarders.

I peddled ice to Stone's Farm and Whitewall Manor up on Route 9 by the entrance to the Poughkeepsie Yacht Club. They were boarding houses for the people from New York. There were a lot of summer visitors who stayed in Staatsburg. It was a different mode of living then. They weren't as mobile. The people would come up and then be rather sedentary. They'd walk or they'd play croquet—just to be in the country and get away from the city, and breathe that good, fresh air. This area was on a main road and it was accessible by train.

Fred Mulford had a garage up on Route 9 where the lawn mower shop is now. I used to deliver ice there. And up where Paula's Restaurant is now, a man by the name of Gene Southerland owned that. It was a restaurant. There was the Cozy Inn down near where the factory is now, and Bud Hess had a place down there, too. Ingalls had the Green Bullfrog, I think. That was another place.

One time at the place up on Route 9 that is now Paula's, I was backing the truck in to deliver ice. It was a Model A Ford rack body. I was standing on the running board, both feet outside the cab, and the door caught on a fence post. The door started to close on my neck and just by luck the fence post broke loose and released me. I went down to Dr. Herridon's in Staatsburg to have my neck checked out.

I peddled ice until I graduated from high school in 1936. Then I went to work on the railroad as a section guy along the track in Staatsburg. I did many tasks when I worked for the railroad. You raised or lowered tracks if it got bumps in it. Run a jackhammer to push the stones under the ties to make them solid. If the ties were rotten, you pulled them out and replaced or re-spiked them. You'd straighten out the rip-rap. Those were the stones the ties sat on and you had to make a straight edge of them along the tracks. John

Andrews was the main foreman, and before my time he used to have the prize section through here. You'd put a board down and you'd scrape all the stone and you'd have a nice straight edge. It was all hard work. It was the coldest place in the wintertime and the hottest place in the summertime. Although we used to sneak off once in awhile and go swimming in the river.

Down at the railroad station in Staatsburg, a man by the name of Stickles was the station agent at that time. A station agent sold tickets, took care of the freight, generally just took care of the station. And there used to be a little bit of a shack on the south side of the railroad crossing where a man stayed, and he came out to put the crossing gates up and down every time a train came through.

I used to work at the station here sometimes, and I remember one time a couple of teachers I had in school came in on the train one morning. They said, "Oliver, what are you doing here?"

I said, "I'm a walking ad for a high school education."

I was a little bitter but well, there weren't any jobs in 1936. Really, I was just happy to have any job.

I was joking with the teachers because I was grateful to have a job. In those days you couldn't buy, beg, or steal a job. That's when Roosevelt started with his alphabet—you had the CCC camps, WPA, PWA, and all those other agencies. The schools were built that way—the two grade schools and Roosevelt High School. You just ride through the countryside and wherever your see a public building that is stone—that was from the Roosevelt era. Post office in Hyde Park, Rhinebeck, Poughkeepsie, Wappingers were all the influence of this public works program.

Another involvement that I had in Staatsburg was with the CCC camp at Norrie Park. They had barracks, a mess shack, and hospital shack up there in the field where the fitness trail is now. After the

CCC moved out, my family moved into one of the buildings up there for awhile as caretakers. I think that was around 1937. The Civilian Conservation Corps was an emergency relief effort. You enlisted to get in. The fellas were paid, I guess probably about 30 dollars a month and room and board. They taught them the trades, they gave them work, they had a place to stay, and I think they got about 6 dollars a month to spend. The rest was sent home for their people. It was one of Roosevelt's efforts to save the economy. The CCC fellas built Norrie Point Inn, they built the roads, the bridges and the camp area on top of the hill at Norrie.

We were sort of the caretakers up there just to keep an eye on the place, protect it from fire. But, the one building we were in caught fire and we had to move to another one! After that we moved back to Hyde Park where I had lived most of my life. They tore all those buildings down. There used to be a big house up at the south end of that big grassy area. That was torn down, too.

Norrie Point was a nice restaurant. My wife and I announced our engagement at a dinner dance there in 1941. Connie Ekstrand ran it then. She was quite a restauranteur. She had run the Vassar Alumni House at one time, and the restaurant at the Vanderbilt Visitor's Center during the war, I think. Norrie had a big fireplace and huge patio with tables. The Cardinal Inn was a very good restaurant, too, after the war. I remember we used to go to the Pleasant Plains Grange Hall. They used to have dances there.

My experience with Franklin Roosevelt living in Hyde Park goes back to when I was a kid and sang in the choir. He would come into church and in those days he was just Franklin Roosevelt. 1923, 24, 25. The fire department created more of a scene going through town than Roosevelt did. As he became governor, you became more aware of him.

The funny thing is, the whole damn town of Hyde Park was Republican and they used to damn him up and down, but they were making money off him; making money off the fact that he was there. The Roosevelt and Vanderbilt Historic Sites have been the biggest industries in Hyde Park for a long time. They bring 200,000-300,000 people a year into this area.

Every election day we used to have a torchlight parade up into the Roosevelt Estate. Whether a local or national election, we'd all meet and light these red torches and parade up to the Roosevelt Home and Roosevelt would come out on the porch and talk to us. In those days it was something to do. NOW it's part of Americana; it's part of history. You lived this history. They don't have torchlight parades anymore.

In fact, I think it was 1936—Cece Marshall was elected by one vote. He was the first Republican road commissioner they had in thirty-some years. Roosevelt came out on the porch and greeted him as "One Vote Marshall." He was known as "One Vote Marshall" from then on.

Oliver Goring

It used to be that on every election day, Ike Van Wagner used to put a half of beer on in several of the barrooms along the way so you'd go from barroom to barroom drinking and dancing and having a good time. Before the election you'd be arguing with everybody and after the election you'd be all out drinking together. Ike was quite a guy that way.

Working at the Roosevelt Home it always amazed me the amount of feeling people continued to have for Roosevelt. People would come to his gravesite and cry and get down on their knees and pray. They really loved him. Some of them thought he was like a God.

www.ingramcontent.com/pod-product-compliance
Lightning Source LLC
Chambersburg PA
CBHW022152080426
42734CB00006B/401